THE EARLIEST
CHRISTIAN CONFESSIONS

OSCAR CULLMANN
Professor at the University of Basel

Translated by
J. K. S. REID

WIPF & STOCK · Eugene, Oregon

Wipf and Stock Publishers
199 W 8th Ave, Suite 3
Eugene, OR 97401

The Earliest Christian Confessions
By Cullmann, Oscar and Reid, J. K. S.
Copyright©1949 James Clarke Lutterworth Press
ISBN 13: 978-1-5326-5336-0
Publication date 3/14/2018
Previously published by Lutterworth Press, 1949

CONTENTS

Note

This book was first published in French, entitled *Les Premières Confessions de Foi Chrétiennes*, Presses Universitaires de France, 1943. In the same year a German edition was published by Evangelischer Verlag A.b. Zollikon, Zürich, entitled *Die ersten christlicher Glaubensbekenntnisse.*

Preface to the 2018 Reprint Edition

By Gary R. Habermas and Benjamin C.F. Shaw

This present volume by Oscar Cullmann first appeared in English in 1949, under the title *The Earliest Christian Confessions*.[1] It had previously been published in French,[2] and then also in German,[3] both in 1943. Though brief, it has often been acclaimed since as the best overall book on the subject of early Christian creeds or confessions. For example, after a survey of German, French, and English titles on this subject, New Testament scholar Richard N. Longenecker referred to this text by Cullmann as, "probably the most significant of all these studies."[4]

This evaluation was brought home to me (Habermas) when, several years ago, I was lecturing in Cambridge, U.K. My assigned topic was philosophical and historical aspects of the contemporary miracles discussion from Schleiermacher to the present, with a couple of hours to draw out some trends and implications, specifically regarding the resurrection of Jesus. Soon after I began the lecture, Richard Bauckham walked in and took a seat.

1. Trans. J.K.S. Reid (London: Lutterworth, 1949).

2. *Les Premières Confessions de Foi Chrétiennes* (Paris: Presses Universitaires de France, 1943).

3. *Die ersten christlicher Glaubensbekenntnisse* (Zürich: Evangelischer Verlag A.b. Zollikon, 1943).

4. Longenecker, *New Wine into Fresh Wineskins: Contextualizing the Early Christian Confessions* (Peabody, MA: Hendrickson, 1999), 14.

After the lecture had ended, I asked Richard for a comment. At first he settled for some kind compliments regarding the address. Pushing a little further, I asked him for any additional thoughts that he might think would be helpful. As I recall, he only added that, in the portion of the lecture where I had discussed the New Testament creeds, he thought that I could have detailed Cullmann's conclusions from this particular volume. I thanked him and smiled, explaining that I had given a very similar invited lecture at Oxford University just days earlier and had indeed spent some time detailing the very text by Cullmann, though I had omitted such on this occasion.

Bauckham's comment more than anything else has served as a reminder of the reputation of Cullmann's volume, that it could be remembered in that manner even more than a half century later! Such is not always the case, even with texts that made a splash in their own day.

Oscar Cullmann was a German-speaking Lutheran who was born in Strasbourg, France in 1902. He attended the University of Strasbourg and in 1930 became a professor there. In 1938 he began teaching at the University of Basel where he taught New Testament and Early Church History. In 1948 he also began teaching Early Christianity at the Sorbonne (University of Paris). He retired in 1972 and continued writing before passing away in 1999.

During his career, Cullmann also contributed a number of other highly influential volumes on topics such as Christology, the early church, along with his pioneer ecumenical discussions between Protestants and Roman Catholics. Some of his most important and influential published texts include *Christ and Time*, *The Christology of the New Testament*, *Salvation in History*, *The Early Church*, and *Immortality of the Soul or Resurrection of the Dead?* (reprinted by Wipf and Stock, 2000).

In the decades prior to and during the early years of Cullman's academic career, the wider world of New Testament scholarship had been preoccupied with studies of what came to be known later as the First Quest of the Historical Jesus. During the nineteenth and early twentieth centuries, German scholarship in particular had become quite critical of what could be ascertained as the historical bedrock of

Jesus' life and teachings. Soon after the dawn of the twentieth century, Albert Schweitzer wrote his famous book, *The Quest of the Historical Jesus*, with a critique that was so devastating[5] and effective, along with other factors, that the "Quest" entered a period where many of the most influential scholars largely abandoned the historical underpinnings of this movement. Out of this atmosphere emerged Karl Barth's early dialectical approach to theology, along with Rudolf Bultmann's existentialist ideology and demythologizing efforts.

Cullmann's academic career began during the intersections of these major theological thoroughfares, overshadowed by Barth and Bultmann along with their critiques of searches for the Jesus of history. Cullmann particularly opposed Bultmann's approach, which he critiqued as distorting the New Testament text and ideas by viewing them only through his modern existentialist categories. Bultmann had little or no use for the ideas that God had acted literally in human history or in special revelation within the world, while focusing on authentic living in the present. Cullmann discovered a closer ally in Barth, especially in their disagreements with Bultmann.

Cullmann was unsatisfied with approaches that neglected the crucial role played by important historical events described in the New Testament and sought to recover the notion of *Heilsgeschichte* (salvation history) in biblical thought. For Cullmann, within the wider scope of history, salvation history was the process whereby God revealed the redemptive plan for persons through past events. Jesus stands at the center of this history, having inaugurated the Kingdom of God.

In Jesus, although the Kingdom of God had already come, it had not yet been manifested in its fullest, most complete sense. This "already but not yet" notion may be understood in a sense similar to the way that a decisive victory in battle may determine that the end of the war is in sight even before that final termination occurs, because the victory essentially signals the inevitable—the coming of the end.

5. Schweitzer, *The Quest of the Historical Jesus: A Critical Study of its Progress from Reimarus to Wrede*, trans. by W. Montgomery, 1906 (New York: Macmillan, 1968), especially 398–403.

So though the battle is not the official end of the war, it signals and even proclaims the victor. Cullmann emphasized that Jesus had already fought and won the battle.

Cullmann, then, was chiefly concerned with God's actions and revelation in history, though generally apart from evidential arguments. This view is presented most fully in his work, *Salvation in History*.[6] Given this interest, it is hardly surprising that Cullmann analyzed similar New Testament themes such as creedal texts, best represented in this treatment in *The Earliest Christian Confessions*. This text was published just shortly before the beginning of the "New Quest for the Historical Jesus" (also called the "Second Quest for the Historical Jesus") though it was not a part of that trend or its ideas.[7]

In examining many of the early New Testament creedal texts, Cullmann's *Early Christian Confessions* was one of the initial volumes that helped contribute to moving scholarship in the direction of a more textual emphasis on the historical nature of Christian origins. An important element during the time of these early first century confessions was that they sought to trace the development (and necessity) of Christian doctrine in summarized form, representing a stage of the oral tradition prior to what often occupied the form critics. Cullmann argued that five different aspects of the *Sitz im Leben* (life setting) would have required the disciples and apostles to develop various creedal formulas: baptism and catechumenism, regular worship, exorcism, persecution, and polemics against heretics.[8]

Due to the early spadework on the confessions provided by Cullmann and other scholars, the importance of early creeds for New Testament studies can hardly be overemphasized today. These creeds actually

6 Cullmann, *Salvation in History*, trans. S.G. Sowers (London: SCM, 1967).

7 Scholars often identify the origins of this newer trend with a 1953 lecture given, curiously enough, by one of Bultmann's own former students, Ernst Käsemann, who thought that his mentor had gone too far in his distrust of historical research regarding Jesus. Käsemann, "The Problem of the Historical Jesus," *Essays on New Testament Themes*, Studies in Biblical Theology (London: SCM, 1964).

8. Cullmann, *The Earliest Christian Confessions*, 18–32.

predate the writings in which they appear, especially as indicated by the frequent introductions which state that the texts were previously derived and passed along from earlier teachers (such as 1 Corinthians 11:2; 11:23a, 15:3a).[9] This creedal research legacy "remains a firmly entrenched axiom of critical scholarship."[10]

In fact, these originally oral texts may be the best answer to the question regarding the state of the earliest Christian beliefs before a single canonical book was written! Moreover, they are crucial witnesses to what was taught from the beginning of Christianity, even *prior* to Paul's conversion.[11] Cullmann held that the confessions dated from the earliest church and were possibly apostolic.[12] Perhaps this is why it has been declared in the most recent research that, "The earliest Christology was already the highest Christology."[13]

The import of these confessions is recognized widely by critical scholars, too. Even skeptical New Testament researchers such as Bart Ehrman,[14] among others,[15] have concluded that a number of the creeds are indeed pre-Pauline in nature, meaning that, by the time that Paul was converted, these confessional sayings had already been in existence beforehand, passed along as apostolic in origin.

---

9. Other examples in the epistles include texts such as 2 Thess. 2:15; 3:6; 1 Tim. 1:15a; 3:1; 4:9-10; 2 Tim. 2:11-13; Titus 1:9; cf. Mk. 7:3b; Lk. 24:34.

10. Longenecker, *New Wine into Fresh Wineskins*, 10.

11. James D.G. Dunn, *Beginning from Jerusalem*, Vol. 2 of *Christianity in the Making* (Grand Rapids, MI: Eerdmans, 2009), especially 105-8.

12. Cullmann, *The Earliest Christian Confessions*, 13, 16, 49-50.

13. Richard Bauckham, *Jesus and the God of Israel: God Crucified and Other Studies on the New Testament's Christology of Divine Identity* (Grand Rapids, MI: Eerdmans, 2008), x, 128-30; cf. 30, 195-210.

14. Bart Ehrman, *Did Jesus Exist? The Historical Argument for Jesus of Nazareth* (New York: Harper Collins, 2012), 111, 130-31, 261-62, 290 for some examples.

15. C.H. Dodd, *The Apostolic Preaching and its Developments* (London: Hodder & Stoughton, 1936; Grand Rapids, MI: Baker, 1980), 16, 18-19, 26, 31; Paul Barnett, *The Birth of Christianity: The First Twenty Years* (Grand Rapids, MI: Eerdmans, 2005), 85; cf. 56; cf. also Longenecker, *New Wine into Fresh Wineskins*, 10, 14, 26.

These are just some of the major reasons why so much is at stake in a study of the early Christian creeds or confessions. Many gems have been discovered from these particular critical analyses that chiefly began almost one hundred years ago.[16] Further development in twentieth and twenty-first century studies have made much progress in this pursuit. To a certain extent, Cullmann's volume *The Earliest Christian Confessions* led the way forward. As such, we are pleased to reintroduce this highly influential study.

16. As in Longenecker's list of texts (*New Wine into Fresh Wineskins*, 9–10).

INTRODUCTION

The Problem

IN the present work we propose to examine the origin of the confessions of faith. Our object is not to sketch a history of the development of the later confessions—that is, of those which in a fixed text served one of the communities of the ancient Church as rule of faith.[1] We occupy ourselves rather with their " pre history ", and ask how, at a time when everything was still fluid, and before certain types of symbol became fixed, the Church came to work out formulas comprehensive of the faith.[2] This prehistory stretches in all over the first century and the second half of the second. But to understand the forces which disclose themselves at this time, we must consider their later development, and from there proceed to the beginnings.

A comment on method is necessary here. This " retrospective " procedure, which has yielded excellent results in the examination of the ancient liturgies,[3] also conceals certain dangers if it is applied in too one-sided a fashion. It has, in fact, directed many works on the specific question which occupies us here into a wrong course.[4] One runs the danger here of wanting to find right at the beginning the germs of facts which only achieved significance later. But it is to be remembered that the initial form of the questions was often quite different from the later.

Thus there are two possible methods: one demanding that in order to examine the origin of a phenomenon we forget its later development; and the other, on the contrary, recommending that we allow ourselves to be taught by the later development, in order to understand better the beginnings. We believe that the two methods ought to be combined here.

Four questions present themselves before us:

1. Why did Christians need to have, besides Scripture, an " apostolic " formula to summarise the faith they professed ?
2. What circumstances brought this necessity about ?
3. What is the composition of the first formulas, and how did they develop in the earliest times ?
4. What is the essential content of the Christian faith according to the earliest formulas ?

[1] At the same time, we shall have frequent occasion to cite these confessions. They are brought together in the collection of August Hahn, *Bibliothek der Symbole und Glaubensregeln der Alten Kirche*, 3rd edn., by Ludwig Hahn, 1897. For the rest, it is hard to draw up a genuine history of the origins of the confessions, especially of the very numerous and diverse symbols of the East (cf. H. Lietzmann, *Symbolstudien, Zeitschrift für die neutestamentliche Wissenschaft*, 1922, p. 24). Certain results, however, of works of the last forty years may be taken as accepted, in so far as they concern the differentiation of the chief " types of symbol ". The work which has been classic for a long time is that of F. Kattenbusch, *Das apostolische Symbol*, 2 vols., 1894-1900. Along with it should be mentioned A. E. Burn, *An Introduction to the Creeds and the Te Deum*, 1899; and F. Loofs, *Symbolik oder christliche Konfessionskunde*, 1902.

All these studies have been reanimated by the exhaustive works of H. Lietzmann, for the most part appearing in the *Zeitschrift für die neutestamentliche Wissenschaft*, under the title " *Symbolstudien* " (*ZNW*, 1922, p. 1 ff.; 1923, p. 257 ff.; 1925, p. 193 ff.; 1927, p. 75 ff.).

For the period of origins, see K. Holl, *Zur Auslegung des 2. Artikels des sogenannten apostolischen Glaubensbekenntnisses* in the *Sitzungsbericht der Berliner Akademie der Wissenschaften*, 1919, p. 2 ff.; A. v. Harnack, *ibid.*, p. 112 ff.; H. Lietzmann, *ibid.*, p. 269 ff.; further, H. Lietzmann, *Die Anfänge des Glaubensbekenntnisses* in the *Festgabe zu A. v. Harnacks 70. Geburtstag*, 1921, p. 226 ff. The same writer also gives a good summary of his point of view in vol. 2 of his *Geschichte der Alten Kirche*, 1936, pp. 100-119.

Independently of Lietzmann, J. Haussleiter examines the question of origins in *Trinitarischer Glaube und Christusbekenntnis in der Alten Kirche*, 1920. He agrees in many points with Lietzmann. R. Seeberg represents a rather divergent view: " *Zur Geschichte der Entstehung des apostolischen Symbols* " in *Zeitschrift für Kirchengeschichte*, New Series, III, 1922, p. 1 ff. Finally, mention should be made of P. Feine, *Die Gestalt des apostolischen Glaubenbekenntnisses in der Zeit des Neuen Testaments*, 1925, a work, however, whose methods and conclusions are rejected by the majority of critics. The chapter which Ethelbert Stauffer in his *Theologie des Neuen Testaments*, 1941, devotes to the question of the confessions (p. 212 ff.), deserves special mention, as does also the brief supplement (III, p. 322) in which he raises the question of the criteria which allow us to distinguish in the New Testament between the confessional formulas and their context. See further p. 20, footnote 1.

² *Mutatis mutandis*, we attempt the same thing as *Formgeschichte* has done for the Gospel tradition. But for the prehistory of the confessions of faith, we stand on an incomparably more certain ground, since we possess the precursors of the future symbols in " written " documents.

³ Cf., *e.g.*, H. Lietzmann, *Messe und Herrenmahl*, 1926.

⁴ Cf. Chapters 2 and 3.

Chapter 1

THE APOSTOLIC CHARACTER OF THE RULE
OF FAITH AND SCRIPTURE

THE Christian Church makes use of two types of confession of faith:

1. The symbol set up once for all, and drawn up in the language of the New Testament. This is ascribed to the apostles as an authentic summary of Scripture.

2. The symbol conditioned by circumstances, which transcribes the Biblical Gospel into the language and concepts of a certain period. On the basis of the New Testament, this symbol takes up position over against new problems and heresies unknown in the apostolic age.[1]

In the creative period which concerns us here the question is how the first type came to be fixed; and there is as yet no reason to make this distinction. The two streams are still mixed, since it is in the contemporary *circumstances* of the apostolic century that the earliest beginnings of the future confessions of faith appear.

Originally the need for an " apostolic " summary was all the greater, since Christian doctrine existed in oral form only. At that time brief symbolic formulas may have been drawn up, probably even before the Gospel tradition was fixed.[2] When the earliest Chris-

---

[1] An example of the first type is the so-called Apostles' Creed, an example of the second, the Nicene. The Niceno-Constantinopolitan symbol represents a mixed type, on the one hand containing the anti-Arian formula, but on the other often regarded as apostolic. (Cf. C. P. Caspari, *Ungedruckte, unbeachtete und wenig beachtete Quellen zur Geschichte des Taufsymbols und der Glaubensregel*, I, 1866, p. 242, No. 45; II, 1869, p. 115, No. 88; III, 1875, p. 12, No. 22.)

[2] This would represent a stage of oral tradition earlier than that which Form Criticism examines in the case of the Gospels.

tian writings appeared between 50 and 150, in a quantity of which the New Testament of today gives only a meagre idea, a doctrinal summary was not less necessary. The Church had not yet made a choice among Christian works; it had not yet accorded to a small number of them the dignity of Holy Scripture and set them beside the Old Testament. For this reason a *summa fidei* was indispensable. This need persisted when, towards the middle of the second century, a number of writings was gradually separated and slowly assembled into the canon of the New Testament. For this canon that was being formed, which in its final shape contained twenty-seven writings, was of too great length to serve as rule of faith. In view of the richness of this compilation and the multiplicity of the writings there assembled, the essential content had to be extracted.

So the question was raised: what is the common core of these traditions, at first transmitted orally and then fixed in written form by such different authors? In this tradition and in these books, what is common core and what particular development? Every confession of faith, whether worked out consciously or originating spontaneously, gives an implicit answer to this question. It is plain that such a task is of great importance and offers considerable difficulties. Anyone who summarizes the Biblical tradition realizes at once the necessity of distinguishing between the central principle and what is derived from it.[1] The whole problem of Scriptural exposition depends on this distinction. What is the standard that allows us to discriminate between these two elements? In the period of primitive Christianity every confession of faith in one way or another proves to be such a standard, even if to give an answer to this question is not its immediate aim.

[1] Hence every theology of the New Testament presupposes a corresponding rule of faith.

Hence the facts mentioned in the symbol possess an outstanding importance in the Church for the understanding of Christian doctrine. The Church has to know whether the symbol really contains what the authors of the twenty-seven books of the New Testament regarded as the essential content of their writings. For example, it is not a matter of indifference for the Church whether the centre of the New Testament, from which all the rest must be judged, is the teaching of Jesus (which is mentioned by none of the ancient symbols[1]), or whether it is rather the facts mentioned in the ancient symbols. If the view is advocated that the teaching of Jesus is the core of the New Testament, as Erasmus held, the New Testament facts enumerated in most of the symbols will be regarded as less essential, and one will expound the New Testament accordingly. But if, on the contrary, the view of the ancient symbols is advocated, the Sermon on the Mount will be explained in the light of the facts enumerated in them. In this case one will emphasize that it is Christ who prescribed these rules; and the words " but I say unto you " will stand in the forefront.

The best known of the ancient confessions of faith, the so-called Apostles' Creed, has often been thus criticized in the Church. The objection was made to it that it did not rightly bring into clear prominence the real centre of the Gospel. Even the orthodox theologians of the seventeeth century dared to attack it. They were offended that in it the Pauline doctrine of justification by faith, which the Reformation had made the principal content of the Gospel, was not once mentioned. On the other hand, it was objected that this symbol raised the miraculous birth of Christ and His descent into hell into essential dogmas, although in the New

---

[1] When Justin accords to Jesus the epithet $\delta\iota\delta\acute{a}\sigma\varkappa\alpha\lambda o\varsigma$ in the formula which he quotes in *Apol.*, I, 13 and 14, this is manifestly an addition, introduced by the apologist himself, and according with his special conception of the work of Christ as the revealer of truth.

Testament these elements stand only on the periphery. Here we have not to enquire whether these critical remarks, directed against the apostolic symbol and for the most part also applicable to the earlier confessions, are well grounded. They do, however, show us how difficult it is to work out a confession of faith, since it involves an exegesis of the whole New Testament.

The ancient Church reckoned seriously with this difficulty. Thus it took the trouble to emphasize the objective character of the rule of faith, and to eliminate every suspicion of arbitrariness. Hence the importance of possessing a formula which was traceable back to the apostles, just as every writing in order to be canonical had to be traceable to an apostle or to the disciple of an apostle.[1] A summary of the essential doctrine of the New Testament in a symbolic document had objective worth only if it could claim the apostles themselves as its authors. Only so did the confession of faith really become the norm, which one could set as key at the beginning of the New Testament, since the Church accorded it an equal authority with the canon. In the second half of the second century, as unanimity was reached about the main lines of the confession of faith, the view spread that the rule of faith was composed by the apostles.[2] Yet its text in the second century was not fixed in the same fashion everywhere, though the *principle* of a common rule was acknowledged. One can even at times find several formulas in one and the same writer.[3] On the other hand, the chief articles of the confession were already settled. The conviction of

---

[1] The desire here was not to set *every* ecclesiastical tradition above Scripture. It was rather a matter of dethroning every *future* tradition in the name of *apostolic* tradition.

[2] Cf. Irenæus: *Adv. Hær.*, I, 10, 1; *ibid.*, III, 4, 1 f.

[3] Cf. Irenæus, *op. cit.*, I, 10, 1 ff., and IV, 33, 7; and even earlier, Ignatius: *ad Trall.*, 9, agreeing with *ad Smyrn.*, 1. Similarly, the New Testament canon was established in its main lines and its principle acknowledged, and yet variations concerning its definitive contents persisted for a long time.

their apostolic composition strengthened the authority of the confession to such a degree that Tertullian traces it back to Christ,[1] and calls it an " oath on the banner of Christ ";[2] and Irenaus can write: " If the apostles had left behind them no writings, it would still have been necessary to follow the rule of faith which they transmitted to the leaders of the Church."[3]

This tradition later gave rise to the naïve legend, according to which every apostle had contributed his share to the text.[4] The most singular form of this tale is the one which explains the origin of the so-called " Apostolicum ", and to which it owes its outstanding dignity. According to this legend, " the disciples were gathered on the tenth day after the Ascension, in fear of the Jews. Then the Lord sent the promised Paraclete to them. On his appearing, they were all inflamed as with glowing iron, and, filled with the knowledge of all languages, they composed the symbol." Then the text relates which sentence or part of a sentence was spoken by each of the twelve.[5] This legend deliberately chose the story of John 20: 10 ff. as framework, since only there did the twelve apostles alone partake of the outpouring of the Holy Spirit. We see, then, how the composition of this symbol is traced back to a direct operation of the Holy Spirit and a collaboration of the twelve apostles. Thus the highest authority was conferred upon it, and the same attributes as distinguish the canon of the New Testament: inspiration by the Holy Spirit, and composition by the apostles.

At the same time, the pretension of the rule of faith to " apostolicity " satisfied the need, which had already manifested itself early, for possessing an attestation

[1] *De Præser. Hær.* 13: " a Christo instituta."
[2] *Adv. Praxeam,* 2, 30.
[3] Irenaus, *Adv. Hær.*, III, 4, 1.
[4] Attested for the first time in *Apostolic Constitutions,* VI, 14. For later citations, see Hahn, *op. cit.,* p. 52, footnote 87.
[5] Cf. Pseudo-Augustine, *Sermones de Symbolo,* 240 (Hahn, p. 50, footnote 86).

14

from the twelve, which should legitimize the content of the canon. The impression of arbitrariness which clung to the choice of twenty-seven New Testament writings was thus mitigated. This impression of arbitrary choice was particularly strong in the case of the Gospels. Instead of a single account of the life of Jesus declared authentic by the twelve, we possess four, of which only two are composed by apostles, the other two being the work of disciples of the apostles.[1] This explains the origin of a Gospel " according to the twelve apostles ", attested by Origen.[2] For this reason, on the other hand, the Muratorian Canon tries to prove that at least the Gospel according to John was composed by the commission and under the supervision of the twelve.[3] This legend expresses the same concern as that about the apostolic symbol.[4] But neither the Gospel " according to the Twelve ", nor the opinion of the Muratorian Canon about the composition of the Johannine Gospel, won acceptance. It was therefore all the more import-

[1] This state of things is the origin of various attempts undertaken in antiquity to replace the *four* Gospels by a single one. Such attempts were made by: Marcion, who recognized one of the four, namely Luke, as alone canonical; the Ebionites, who had only the Gospel according to Matthew (Irenæus, *op. cit.*, III, 11, 7); Basilides, Theophil of Antioch (cf. Jerome, *Epist.*, 121, 6, 15), and Tatian, who all compiled Harmonies of the Gospels, of which Tatian's Harmony has been preserved. The trouble which Irenæus (*op. cit.*, III, 11, 8) took to justify the number of the Gospels shows us that a genuine problem was seen here. See also O. Cullmann, *Die Pluralität der Evangelien als theologisches Problem in Altertum*, Theologische Zeitschrift, Basel, 1945, p. 23 ff.

[2] Origen, *In Lucam Homiliæ*, 1, and Jerome, *In Matth. Intr.* and *Contra. Pelag.*, III, 2. Cf. with this H. Waitz in ZNW, 1913, p. 45 ff. Much later, we find a " Gospel of the Twelve Apostles " in Syria. (Cf. Rendel Harris, Cambridge, 1900.)

[3] *Canon Muratori* (cf. E. Preuschen, *Analecta*, 1910, p. 129 ff.): " John, one of the disciples, to the entreaties of the other disciples and bishops, answered: 'Fast with me from today for three days, and what is then revealed to each we shall do together.' The same night it was revealed to Andrew, one of the apostles, that John should write out everything under his own name, and all the rest should check it."

[4] Similarly it should be mentioned that the Ecclesiastical Constitutions are ascribed to the twelve apostles, the Didache offering the earliest example of such attribution.

15

ant to possess a *rule of faith* guaranteed by the authority of the apostles.

The legend about the apostolic symbol, diffused through all the Middle Ages, was destroyed in the fifteenth century[1] by the Humanist, Laurentius Valla.[2]

We know to-day that the apostolic symbol in its present form reaches back no further than the seventh or sixth century, and that its predecessor, the ancient baptismal symbol of Rome, and the kindred symbols of East and West, go back to the second century, but not into the apostolic period. Can apostolic dignity be claimed, nevertheless, for the earliest beginnings, that is for the confessions of faith of the first century, which we will examine here ? We should then in spite of all have at our disposal a certain norm, an *apostolic* summary of Christian doctrine.

It is clear that "apostolicity", in the sense of the composition of a certain precise formula by certain apostles, must be given up even in the case of the very earliest confessions. Yet the bulk of them will lead us back into apostolic *times*. The formulas of the first century present themselves, if not as the work of "the apostles" themselves, at all events as the work of the *Church of the apostolic age*. But in this case it is im-

---

[1] In an explanation of the symbol ascribed to St. Bernard (cf. Hahn, *op. cit.*, p. 53, footnote 87), the contribution of each of the apostles is given in hexameters, the better to imprint it on the memory:

> *Articuli fidei sunt bis sex corde tenendi,*
> *Quos Christi socii docuerunt, pneumate pleni:*
> Credo Deum Patrem, *Petrus inquit,* cuncta creantem,
> *Andreas dixit:* Ego credo Jesum fore Christum.
> Conceptum, natum *Jacobus,* Passumque *Johannes,*
> Infera *Philippus* fugit, *Thomasque* revixit.
> Scandit *Bartholomæus,* Veniet censere *Matthæus.*
> Pneuma *minor Jacobus, Simon* peccata remittit.
> Restituit carnem *Judas,* vitamque *Mathias.*

[2] Luther agreed with him, but hesitatingly. For he felt the need of the Church to possess at least *one* confession—which by its composition could claim an equal authority with the New Testament.

16

portant to know the concrete circumstances which gave rise to these formulas. In this way we shall be in a position to judge the objective worth attributable to these most ancient summaries of the Christian Gospel.

Chapter 2

CIRCUMSTANCES OF THE APPEARANCE AND EMPLOYMENT OF THE RULES OF FAITH

WE want now to try to discover the external circumstances which made necessary the use of a rule of faith in the earliest days of the ancient Church. In this way we shall settle what place the rule of faith occupied in the life of the community. This is to apply a technical expression (*Sitz im Leben*), dear to Biblical critics, to the earliest confessions of faith, regarding them as collective products of the apostolic age. It is a common error to suppose forthwith that only *one* external cause is at work. Formerly it was thought that the first confessions owed their origin to the polemical intentions and dogmatic disputes of the primitive Church alone. To-day their origin is ascribed too exclusively to liturgical needs.[1] The fact is that several simultaneous causes contributed to bring about the principles stated in the foregoing chapter, and to extract a confession of faith out of the total Christian tradition. These circumstances can in fact be traced back to the earliest times, even to the New Testament.

We believe it possible to affirm five simultaneous causes, which for the sake of clarity are named forthwith:

1. Baptism and catechumenism;
2. Regular worship (liturgy and preaching);
3. Exorcism;
4. Persecution;
5. Polemic against heretics.

[1] Particularly H. Lietzmann in the above-mentioned studies. In *ZNW*, 1923, p. 262, however, he recognizes in principle that the occasions on which a confession was formulated were various.

Since we are dealing with simultaneous manifestations in the life of the most primitive community, it is generally impossible to ascertain whether a formula owes its first draft to one circumstance more than another. But it is possible to show that any one formula corresponds more particularly to this or that given situation.

1. If we start from the later use of the symbols, we have to think first of all of baptism. In the second century, Irenæus already speaks (*Adv. Hær.*, I, 9, 4) of the " rule of truth " received in baptism.[1] In the light of what has been said, it would be wrong to suppose for this reason alone that every confession since the first century is a *baptismal confession*. Many investigators have fallen into this error.[2] But it is true that in the New Testament baptism was, if not the first, at least the most frequent occasion for *reciting* a symbol. One can deduce from the text of the Acts that at this time a form of rudimentary baptismal liturgy existed. The person baptized, or the person bringing him to baptism, put the question, already stereotyped in the New Testament: *Τί κωλύει;* " Is there any ground for opposing the baptism of this or that candidate ?"[3] On the occasion of the baptism of the Ethiopian eunuch (Acts 8: 36-38), the order of the liturgy appears quite plainly: the eunuch himself asks whether any hindrance to baptism exists. In verse 37 (lacking in one series of manuscripts but particularly well attested in the Western text),[4] Philip gives an answer which appears

---

[1] Cf. also Tertullian, *de Corona Mil.*, 3.
[2] Especially R. Seeberg in the article mentioned above, p. 8, *n.* 1 (*ZKG*, 1922), and P. Feine, *Die Gestalt des apostolischen Glaubensbekenntnisses*, 1925.
[3] Cf. O. Cullmann, *Urchristentum und Gottesdienst*, 1944.
[4] This reading is rejected by most investigators. But even so, we have here a *very ancient* interpolation; for in its brevity this symbol resembles none of the formulas known in the second and third centuries. Hence verse 37 cannot forthwith be regarded as a late gloss. One can indeed

already to have a liturgical character: "If thou believest with all thine heart, thou mayest [be baptised]".
Then the eunuch pronounces his confession of faith:
"I believe that Jesus Christ is the Son of God." This is
one of the most ancient confessions of faith which we
know.

The obligation to confess one's faith in a prescribed
form appears in another passage of the New Testament,
which cites a community formula[1] (1 Peter 3: 18-22).
There we find the chief declarations which we meet in
the second article of the later symbol: Christ died for
us, descended to the "spirits in prison", was raised,
ascended into heaven, sits at the right hand of God. . . .
The preaching to the spirits in prison gives occasion for
the mention of baptism; the text of the confession of
faith is as it were interrupted by a brief instruction on
baptism. This shows that, probably from this time on,
this symbol was used on such occasions.

A confession which mentions Christ and God at the
same time is presupposed in Ephesians 4: 5; and the
introduction of the words " *one* baptism " also indicates
the same particular use.

The rather more developed christological formula
found in Ignatius (*ad. Smyrn.*, 1) numbers His baptism
by John among the outstanding facts in the life of
Jesus. Here we meet again with the same important
concern, to allude to the liturgical act which was the
occasion of the recitation of the confession.

---

ask whether this verse was not omitted in later times because it diverged
from the confessions remaining in use. However this may be, it attests
the use of a baptismal confession at a very early time.

[1] The authors of the New Testament generally do not expressly say
when they make a citation. Only the confession of 1 Cor. 15: 3-7 is
preceded by an introduction in which the apostle Paul explains that it
has been transmitted to him. In other cases, the context and a certain
rhythm allow us to discern the citation. E. Stauffer in his *Theologie des
N.T*, 1941, App. III, p. 322, gives, in rather too rigid a form, twelve
criteria of the contents of the formulas of faith in the New Testament.
The first four and the last of Stauffer's criteria are particularly worth
consideration.

Justin Martyr in his first *Apology* (chap. 61) mentions brief formulas which were to be spoken " in the water ", with invocation of the trinitarian name. Tertullian says expressly that the baptised confesses his faith as he " goes down into the water ",[1] and he informs us that this occurs in the form of question and answer.[2] Later we ascertain that the developed confession of faith has its fixed place at several points in the baptismal ceremony.[3] *Traditio et redditio symboli* took place before baptism; and during the liturgical action the celebrant puts to the candidate the questions taken from the confession of faith, which Tertullian mentions, to each of which the candidate answers: *Credo.*

A baptismal questionnaire (*interrogatio de fide*)[4] from the third century has been preserved: " Dost thou believe with thy whole heart in God almighty, the Father, Creator of all things visible and invisible ?— I believe.—And in Jesus Christ, His Son ?—I believe.— Born of the Holy Ghost and the Virgin Mary ?—I believe.—And in the Holy Ghost, one holy catholic (universal) Church, the forgiveness of sins, the resurrection of the body ? And Palmatius (the candidate), moved to tears, cried: Lord, I believe.''

So the symbol became the foundation of the catechetical instruction preceding Baptism.[5]

2. The need to confess one's faith according to a fixed text manifested itself in every gathering of the community. The believer wants to confess with the brethren before God what unites them before Him. It was already so in the worship of the synagogue, where one, in pronouncing the *Shema*, confessed with all

---

[1] *De Spectaculis,* 4.
[2] *De Corona Mil.,* 3.
[3] Cf. the *Syriac Didascalia* and the *Apostolic Constitutions,* especially Bk. VII, 39-45; and further the Catechisms of Cyril of Jerusalem.
[4] Cf. Hahn, *op. cit.,* parag. 31 a, p. 34.
[5] Cf. A. Seeberg, *Der Katechismus der Urchristenheit,* 1903.

Israel that Yahwe is *one*.[1] The confession of faith is pronounced within the *liturgy* at every *divine service* of the primitive Christian community. In taking account of the later use of the Christian confession in the *Church Order of Hippolytus*,[2] we have especially to think of the eucharistic liturgy.[3]

One of the first confessions of faith composed for the worship of the primitive community is without doubt the text cited by Paul (Phil. 2: 6-11), which has rightly been called a Christian psalm. Paul is not its author; he has only taken it over from the community. It is a hymn, a confession of Christ in rhythmic form, whose original is probably Aramaic.[4] It mentions the " kenosis " of Christ and His appearance " as a common man ", His abasement to the death of the cross, and His exaltation; and it concludes with the proclamation of the present lordship of the glorified Christ: " Wherefore God also hath highly exalted him, and given him a name which is above every name: that at the name of Jesus every knee should bow, of things in heaven, and things in earth, and things under the earth; and every tongue should confess that Jesus Christ is Lord, to the glory of God the Father." The word " confess ", ἐξομολογεῖσθαι, is a deliberate quotation from Isaiah 45: 23; and the conclusion, the culminating point of the whole confession, " Jesus Christ is Lord ", is spoken at the same time by all beings in heaven, on earth and under the

---

[1] The *Shema*, constructed from Deut. 6: 4-9; 11: 13-21, and Num. 15: 37-41, represents indeed more than a confession of faith. Cf. E. Schürer, *Geschichte des jüdischen Volkes im Zeitalter Jesu Christi*, II, pp. 377 and 382, 2nd edn., 1886, and J. Elbogen, *Der jüdische Gottesdienst*, 3rd edn., 1931. Cf. also G. Procksch, *Das Bekenntnis im Alten Testament*, 1936.

[2] Latin text by E. Hauler in *Didascaliæ Apostolorum Fragmenta Veronensia Latina: accedunt Canonum qui dicuntur Apostolorum et Ægyptorum Reliquiæ*, Leipzig, 1900, I, p. 106.

[3] Cf. also *Const. Ap.*, VII, 36, 8.

[4] Cf. E. Lohmeyer, Κύριος Ἰησοῦς, *Sitzungsbericht der Heidelberger Akademie der Wissenschaften*, Phil-Hist. Kl., 1927-28. Cf. also J. Hering, *Le Royaume de Dieu et sa venue*, Paris, 1937, p. 159 ff., who also suggests an Aramaic original, whose source he seeks in the Syrian Church.

earth. Everything said of Christ earlier in the confession belongs rightly to a confession culminating in this concluding formula. We shall see later that this formula was *in itself* a brief confession of faith.

In New Testament times there appears to have been no fixed and universal text for this christological confession. For worship and preaching, or for the instruction of catechumens, one probably used the confession already quoted from Paul in 1 Corinthians 15: 3-7, which, he expressly says, was transmitted to him by the primitive Church, and which he had already taught to the Corinthians—"first of all", indeed, that is, in his *missionary preaching* and his catechetical instruction. It mentions likewise the great Christological events: Christ died for our sins, according to the Scriptures, was buried, and was raised the third day according to the Scriptures; and there then follows a stereotyped enumeration of the various appearances of Christ.[1]

While the hymn of Philippians 2: 6-11 was used as an independent liturgical piece, the confession of 1 Corinthians 15: 3-7 seems to have been employed chiefly in preaching and instruction. However this may be, there was no uniform formula, any more than there was in later centuries a unified text. Yet in the texts cited, the same great christological events appear.

3. A less frequent but very ancient use of the confession of faith is its employment in *exorcism*, attested by Justin (*Dial.*, 30, 3). Here also a confession of faith in Christ has to be pronounced, " to expel and subjugate the demons in the name of the Son of God, the first-born of all creation, who was born of a Virgin, made a passible man, crucified under Pontius Pilate, dead,

[1] Paul added verse 8 to the text current in the Church. He takes up the word ἔκτρωμα, which is probably an insult directed at him on the part of the Jewish Christians, who regarded his apostolate as of secondhand origin.

rose from the dead, ascended into heaven " (*Dial.*, 85, 2). In one place (*Dial.*, 76, 6) the conjuration of " all demons and evil spirits " is effected in the name of " our Lord Jesus, crucified under Pontius Pilate ".

The confession of the Kyrios, of the Lord, of the kingship of Christ, must have had a special significance in exorcisms; for in virtue of the title " Lord ", which belongs to God alone but has been conferred upon Christ (Phil. 3: 10), He is master over all invisible powers and consequently over the world of the demons. We shall see[1] that the express mention of the victory of Christ over the demons, powers and authorities belongs to all the earliest confessions up to the year 150. This must be connected with the employment of the rules of faith in exorcisms. Thus Justin defines the title Kyrios, in a passage which alludes to confession and exorcism: Κύριος τῶν δυνάμεων (*Dial.*, 85, 1).[2]

Justin wrote about 150. The recitation of a confession of faith in an exorcism is, however, older, and goes back to the apostolic age. This is attested by Acts 3: 6, where Peter says to the lame man: " In the name of Jesus Christ the Nazorene, rise up and walk." This formula, in which the words " Christ " and " Nazorene "[3] are to be understood in their full mean-

---

[1] Chapter 4.

[2] Origen later recalls (*Contra Celsum*, I, 6 and I, 22) that the Christians owe their power over the demons to the invocation of the name of Jesus, combined with mention of incidents of His life.

[3] It is interesting to meet with the probably very ancient epithet " Nazorene " in just this exorcist formula (so in Acts 4: 10 in the same context). To derive this designation from the town Nazareth involves considerable philological difficulties (cf. Commentaries to Matt. 2: 23) It is perhaps originally connected with the Semitic root *nathar*, observer (cf. M. Lidzbarski, *Mandäische Liturgien*, Berlin, 1920, p. xvi, and *Ginza*, p. ix. Further, R. Bultmann, " *Die Bedeutung der neuerschlossenen mandäischen Quellen für das Verständnis des Johannesevangeliums*," *ZNW*, 1925, p. 100 ff.).

To us it seems very important that the later exorcisms also contain just this epithet. Cf. *Didasc.*, VI, 23, 8; *Const. Ap.*, VI, 30, 8; *Missale gothicum*, Mabillon, 248, and the Syrian inscription of Refâdeh of 613 (in *Publications of an American Archæol. Expedition to Syria*, Pt. III, 1908, inscription 120, cited by H. Lietzmann, *ZNW*, 1923, p. 267).

ing, and not as proper names, then develops into a proper confession of faith. First in the speech of Peter to the people (3: 13-16), the miracle is ascribed to the "name" of Him who was "delivered" to the Jews, "denied before Pilate", "killed", and "raised by God from the dead". Then in Peter's speech to the priests (4: 10), the same miracle is again ascribed to the name of Jesus Christ "the Nazorene", who was "crucified" by the Jews, and "raised by God from the dead".

It ought also to be noticed that according to the Synoptics the demons themselves bear witness to Christ at their conjuration. In Mark 1: 24 the demon says: "I know thee who thou art, the Holy One of God." In Mark 3: 11 the unclean spirits confess: "Thou art the Son of God." In Mark 5: 7 the demon will himself conjure Christ, since he will have nothing to do with Him, and he testifies to Him: "Jesus, thou Son of the most high God, I adjure thee. . . ."

4. When we pay heed to the Greek words in the New Testament and primitive Christian literature bearing the meaning "confess", ὁμολογέω and μαρτυρέω, we discover how often they are employed in connection with *persecutions*.[1] To such an extent does this occur, that μαρτυρέω acquired the meaning "suffer martyrdom". It is all the more astonishing that studies of the origins of the confessions of faith take almost no account of persecutions. We must particularly cite the words about confession in the two Epistles to Timothy, and especially 1 Timothy 6: 12-16 and the important verse 13: "I give thee charge in the sight of God, who quickeneth all things, and before Christ Jesus, who before Pontius Pilate witnessed a good confession, that thou keep this commandment without spot, unrebukable. . . ." The whole context proves

[1] Cf. for ὁμολογία F. Kattenbusch, *Das apostolische Symbol*, II, 1900, p. 283.

that we are here concerned with a judicial action, and that Timothy had appeared already for the first time before a court, and " had witnessed a good confession before many witnesses ".[1] He is to continue the " good fight ", that is confess his faith before the authorities, which demands much courage and faith. He is to do it as Jesus did before Pontius Pilate, and is to mention this fact in his confession. Pilate probably owes the honour of being named in the Credo to the fact that Christians of the early period were summoned to confess their faith before the representatives of the Roman government. In this situation it was a strength to their courage to remember that Christ had proclaimed His messianic kingship before Pilate. So they spoke of the *confessing* Christ in the confession pronounced in persecutions.

Why did Christ *confessing* before Pontius Pilate become Christ *suffering* under Pontius Pilate in the symbol?[2] It is the consequence of the other causes examined here which contributed to the formation of the symbol. In those other circumstances it was even more important to remember the Christ who " suffered under Pontius Pilate ". There is this reason besides that the word μαρτυρέω, rightly applied in 1 Timothy 6: 13, later acquired the sense " suffer martyrdom ".

[1] P. Feine, *Die Gestalt des apostolischen Glaubensbekenntnisses in der Zeit des Neuen Testamentes*, 1925, makes this text the starting point of his construction. But he wrongly regards it as a baptismal confession. So, too, H. Lietzmann, *ZNW*, 1923, pp. 269 and 271. One ought also to avoid speaking of an " ordination confession," as even J. Jeremias does in *Das Neue Testament Deutsch, ad loc*. That this whole passage refers to persecutions seems to me to have been proved by G. Baldensperger in his study: " *Il a rendu témoignage devant Ponce-Pilate* " (*RHPR*, 1922, pp. 1 ff. and 95 ff.).

[2] H. Lietzmann, *ZNW*, 1923, p. 269, on the contrary, regards μαρτυρήσαντος as secondary to an original σταυρωθέντος. Besides the reasons indicated above for an original μαρτυρήσαντος, it is also to be remembered that at the beginning of the second century the formula " crucified under Pontius Pilate " was not yet fixed. Thus Ignatius writes in the above-mentioned confession *ad Trall.*, 9: ἐδιώχθη; in *ad Smyrn.*, 1: καθηλωμένον.

26

But that the origin of the mention of Pontius Pilate in the symbol is really traceable to the confessing Christ we believe to be proved, indirectly but certainly, in the text cited above, Acts 3: 13.[1] We have affirmed that the reference here is to a fragment of a confession of faith cited at an exorcism. Peter says to the Jews that the miracle in fact occurred through the name of Jesus, whom "ye denied in the presence of Pilate". The original connection between the mention of Pontius Pilate and the confession of Christians reminds Peter that the Jews did the opposite of confess: they denied Jesus.

I Timothy 6: 13 certainly presupposes a more extended confession, in which mention of the confession of Christ forms only one member. It must have already contained the first article, which is rather rare in the symbolical formulas of the New Testament. In fact, we have before us here a plainly bipartite formula: " in the sight of God, who quickeneth all things, and before Christ Jesus, who before Pontius Pilate witnessed a good confession."

The allusion to Pontius Pilate in this confession of persecution is enough to show that the emphasis lies on the second article. Just as *Christ had then proclaimed His kingship*, so must believers confess this kingship of Christ.

In the persecutions, this was the decisive affirmation. But to the same effect the Christians used another very brief and ancient formula, which we have already come across: " Jesus Christ is Lord." This was especially denounced, for the Roman state demanded from its Christian subjects the civic confession consisting of two words: *Κύριος Καῖσαρ*.[2] It is possible that the formula

[1] See p. 25.

[2] A. Deissmann, *Licht vom Osten*, 4th edn., 1923, p. 238, note 3, sees in the number 616, which is quite well attested in Rev. 13: 18, besides 666 (C, arm, Ir.), the secret number, in which this civic confession is concealed under the form *Καῖσαρ Θεός*. The remark in verse 18, *ἀριθμὸς γὰρ ἀνθρώπου ἐστίν*, would fit this exposition very well: a man, whose divinity one must confess.

Kyrios Christos was first fashioned in time of persecution and in opposition to the *Kyrios Kaisar*. But we have already found this confession in the liturgy at a very early time, namely at the end of the hymn of Philippians 2: 6-11, and later in the confessions employed in exorcisms.

In any case, persecution fixed this confession in its stereotyped form. The title of *Kyrios* is the supreme attribute possible, since it belongs to God alone (Heb. *adonai*), and since God Himself conferred it on Christ. Hence the confession of *Kyrios Christos* for the Christian excludes all acknowledgment of another *Kyrios*: Cæsar cannot be *Kyrios*.

For the sake of this brief formula Christians suffered martyrdom. The heathen could not comprehend how Christians could show themselves so narrow-minded, and why they would at no price say *Κύριος Καῖσαρ*. Thus the imperial official remarked to the aged Polycarp of Smyrna, when he appeared before him: "What then is so terrible in saying *Κύριος Καῖσαρ*, and in sacrificing?"[1] What prevented Christians was their firm conviction that there was only one *Κύριος*, the *Κύριος Χριστός*. This brief formula, Christ is Lord, characterised *every* Christian confession of faith. Romans 10: 9 proves this. The matter here concerns faith and confession, and the *Κύριος Ἰησοῦς* is here the object of all confession: If thou confess with thy mouth: Jesus is Lord. . . .[2]

Starting from here, we think it possible to connect with persecution another passage of the New Testament which contains the confession *Κύριος Χριστός*. The passage is 1 Corinthians 12: 3, though, it is true, no one

---

[1] *Mart. Polyc.*, 8, 2. Cf. also Tertullian, *de Corona Mil.*, 11: " Do you believe that it is permitted to a Christian to add an oath made before a man to an oath made before God, and to engage himself to yet another lord after he has once engaged himself to Christ?"

[2] Similarly faith is defined throughout as faith in the *Kyrios*: 1 Cor. 1: 2; Col. 2: 6; Acts 2: 36, 9: 35, 11: 17, 11: 20, 16: 31, 20: 21.

has so interpreted the text. " Wherefore I give you to understand that no man speaking by the Spirit of God calleth Jesus accursed: and that no man can say that Jesus is the Lord, but by the Holy Ghost." This text is found at the beginning of the expositions about spiritual gifts, and is in the main connected with speaking with tongues.[1] But since it is a general introduction, there is no necessity to connect it with speaking with tongues. Besides, speaking with tongues is an inarticulate speech, while here the reference is to a quite precise affirmation. Now the inspiration of the Holy Spirit was announced to the disciples with reference to *times of persecution* (Matt. 10: 17-20, especially verse 19): " When they deliver you up, take no thought how or what ye shall speak: for it shall be given you in that same hour what ye shall speak. For it is not ye that speak, but the Spirit of your Father which speaketh in you." On the other hand, we read in the description of the martyrdom of Polycarp,[2] and especially in the letter of the governor Pliny to Emperor Trajan,[3] that the Christians were ordered by the authorities to curse Christ expressly. It was not sufficient to sacrifice and to say Κύριος Καῖσαρ; the Christians had further to say ἀνάθεμα Χριστός. This fact seems to us to throw a clear light on our text, 1 Corinthians 12: 3. Strengthened by the promise that the Holy Spirit would give the persecuted what he must answer to the authorities, it will be found that several, who had lost courage and abjured in the words " cursed be Jesus ", afterwards offered the excuse that the Spirit had given them this word. Against the intention of these people, Paul

[1] So also H. Lietzmann, *ZNW*, 1923, p. 262.
[2] *Mart. Polyc.*, 9, 3: Polycarp said: " How could I curse (βλασφημῆσαι) my King, who has saved me ?"
[3] Cf. H. Keil's edition, Teubner, Leipzig, 1870, parag. 5: " After they had worshipped thy image with incense and wine, and besides cursed Christ (*maledicerent Christo*)." Parag. 6: " All worshipped thy image and the images of the gods, and cursed Christ (*Christo maledixerunt*)."

29

explains that the Spirit promised to the persecuted is only at work where the confession Κύριος Ἰησοῦς is pronounced. Whoever abjures Christ in this situation proves that he has not the promised Spirit.

We believe, then, that the very ancient citation of this formula indicates to us its employment in persecution. That there were conflicts with the authorities even in Paul's time we know from 2 Corinthians and Acts, especially 17: 7, where those brought by Paul to the faith are accused by the Jews before the civic authorities in the following terms: " These all do contrary to the decrees of Cæsar, *announcing another King, Jesus.*" This shows the clear opposition between *Kyrios Christos* and *Kyrios Kaisar*.[1]

5. The interests of *polemic* led later to fixed and amplified confessions of the second type which we distinguished at the beginning of this work.[2] But its influence was already felt earlier in the formation of confessions of faith of the apostolic type. The struggle against heresies is not strange to the New Testament. It is in fact one of the important reasons occasioning the elaboration of a confession of faith. Among the writings of the period with which we are here occupied it is necessary to give a special place to the letters of the martyr Ignatius of Antioch. He had to combat the Docetists, who maintained that Christ as a divine being had only the appearance of a body. To the refutation of this heresy we owe the confessions which

[1] Even if we did not know this text, we should see no reason why Christians should not have come into conflict with the authorities, and been summoned by them to abjure Christ. We regard as too hard and fast the current opinion, according to which Christianity in its beginnings enjoyed the privileges of Jewry, in the sense that there were at this time no collisions with the state.

The whole Neronic persecution would be incomprehensible, unless the Roman State had come to know the Christians earlier. It was on the basis of previous experiences of them that they were declared state enemies.

[2] See above, p. 10.

Ignatius transmits to us in various passages of his writings.[1] He there lays emphasis on everything which in his view can prove the reality of the carnal body of Christ:[2] " Jesus Christ, of the stem of David, Son of Mary, was really born, ate and drank, really suffered under Pontius Pilate, was really crucified, died in the presence of heavenly, earthly and subterranean beings. He was really raised from the dead. . . ."[3] We see that Ignatius uses an already existent formula, and gives it point against heresy by making additions, especially by the expression " really ". Since there was no uniform text, this was an easy matter. While Ignatius employs a summary already fixed *in content*, his example shows us how certain phrases in the symbol appear as consequences of polemic. The phrase " he ate and drank " vanished later because it proved superfluous.[4] Other parts, on the other hand, which owed their introduction into the symbol to the anti-Docetic struggle, have persisted.

The anti-Docetic struggle goes back to the New Testament, which also took up position against these heretics. It is then not surprising that the anti-Docetic polemic influenced the formation of the confession of

---

[1] *ad Trall.*, 9, and *Smyrn.*, 1; so also *Magn.*, 11, and *Eph.*, 18, 2.

[2] It should be remarked that for him the Virgin Birth was proof of the humanity of Jesus; note especially the very concrete expression of Eph. 18: 2: ἐκυοφορήθη. It is thus not possible to assert that the Virgin Birth of the symbol in the earliest times implied emphasis on the divinity of Christ, and served to prove His humanity only since the Nicene-Constantinopolitan and Chalcedonian symbols. So F. Ménégoz, in his interesting article: " *Engendrement éternel et naissance virginale* " (*RHPR*, 1940, p. 105 ff.). On the contrary, the Virgin Birth, when first mentioned in a symbol, as by Ignatius, is cited precisely to emphasise the humanity of Christ against the Docetists.

[3] *ad Trall.*, 9.

[4] The doctrine of the Gnostic Valentinus, whose Christology was Docetic, shows us that the phrase "He ate and drank", which is grounded in the New Testament, must have played a very important rôle in anti-Docetic polemic. Valentinus will maintain his doctrine of body of pure appearance, and at the same time take account of the fact that Jesus ate and drank: Jesus certainly did this, but no digestive processes took place in Him (Clement, *Stromata*, III, 6, 59).

faith, and that we find a brief anti-Docetic formula already present in the New Testament, stamped as a " confession of faith " by the introductory word ὁμολογεῖν. It is to be found in the First Epistle of John, a work entirely directed against Docetism. The contents of this confession are (1 John 4: 2): " Jesus Christ is come in the flesh."

Elsewhere in the New Testament we find traces of formulas which owe their existence to polemic. Thus the most ancient bipartite formula in 1 Corinthians 8: 6 is directed against heathenish polytheism: " *one* God, the Father, of whom are all things, and we in him; and *one* Lord Jesus Christ, by whom are all things, and we by him." The context of this formula, which deals with things offered to idols, plainly shows that the transition from the ancient formula " Jesus Christ is Lord " to the bipartite confession is the result of opposition to heathenism, where there are many gods and many *Kyrioi*.[1]

Similarly, the confession, 1 Corinthians 15: 3-8, already mentioned, which, as we have seen, was used in preaching and instruction, shows signs also of polemical employment. Paul cites it in the First Epistle to the Corinthians in the course of a refutation of those who denied the resurrection. The especially strong emphasis with which the appearances are mentioned perhaps shows that this confession was formerly also a reply to doubt concerning resurrection. The mention of the fact that Christ was buried, in an otherwise so concise text, certainly answers to a Jewish objection of the kind presupposed in Matthew 28: 18, according to which the disciples had stolen the body of Christ. In this we have the proof that, long before the composition of the Gospels, the certainty of the resurrection was grounded not only on the appearances, but equally on the " empty tomb ".

[1] Cf. O. Weinreich, *Neue Urkunden zur Serapisreligion*, 1919, and E. Peterson, *Εἷς Θεός*, Dissertation, 1920.

The example of I Corinthians 15: 3-18 shows that the same confession was employed on *different* occasions even in New Testament times. Thus we have found the confession Κύριος Ἰησοῦς Χριστός in persecution as well as in worship and exorcism. From this it follows, as we remarked at the beginning of this chapter, that it is not always possible, by ascertaining how it was employed, to conclude that this or that formula was thought out on this or that occasion. Yet we have learnt to distinguish better the grounds on which this or that phrase finally entered the confession of faith as an integral element. The results obtained up till now we shall have to reconsider in the next chapter, where we shall try to demonstrate the development of the structure of these formulas in the earliest age.

The affirmation that several circumstances contributed to the formation of the confessions of faith should prevent us from postulating *a priori* any unified and uniform formula of faith in New Testament times. There were at first different formulas for the different requirements of the Church; each sought in the whole Christian tradition what appeared essential to the end in view. But since a formula originating, for example, in persecution, found employment also in worship and polemic, the road opened for a progressive unification and fusion, such as can be already affirmed of the New Testament age. At this time, one felt the need of a summary of the doctrine of the apostles adequate for all these situations.

As we are able to trace all essential causes back to the New Testament, we regard what was written at the beginning of Chapter I as confirmed.[1] The two motives for the formation of a symbol which were there distinguished, " apostolicity " and " transcription in ac-

[1] See above, p. 10.

cordance with contemporary conditions ", coincide in the primitive age. This results from the fact that the needs of the day, baptism, worship, exorcism, persecution, and polemic, all already characterize the apostolic period. If the summary of the apostolic preaching of this primitive age was conditioned by the different circumstances in which the Church found itself, we can say that the *diverse manifestations of the life of the primitive community* are the criterion of this summary. In the choice made from the total tradition, the life of the New Testament Church is reflected. It is not the apostles, but rather the *community of the apostolic age,* which drew out of the preaching of the Church the facts which we have ascertained in the different formulas, and which correspond to the different mainfestations of its life.

Chapter 3

THE STRUCTURE OF THE ANCIENT FORMULAS AND
THEIR DEVELOPMENT

WE have seen how in New Testament times there is a multiplicity of formulas corresponding to the multiplicity of circumstances which led to a confession of faith being drawn up. On the other hand, we have pointed out that on the same occasion different formulas were employed.[1] We must now examine the *formal* structure of these confessions, pursue their development in the earliest period, and note especially how the multiplicity of circumstances influenced the development.[2]

Here we must above all guard against the temptation to trace the later situation back to primitive times, and to suppose that the tripartite formula was from the beginning alone possible, as though one could speak of a symbol only from the time when the tripartite construction appeared.[3] Thus it is not correct to suppose that the writers of the New Testament and of the ancient Church were speaking only of one *part* of a tripartite confession when they spoke of Christ alone.

In fact, it is rather the analogy of the invocation of the " name " over the baptized in the New Testament that indicates the direction in which the solution to the formal problem of the confession lies.[4] In one text

---

[1] Hence the reconstruction of a uniform New Testament formula, such as P. Feine, *Die Gestalt des Apostolischen Glaubensbekenntnisses,* 1925, has attempted, and more cautiously R. Seeberg in the article mentioned above (*ZKG*, 1922, p. 2 f.), is *a priori* more than questionable.

[2] The question of the doctrinal content common to most of the confessions of this time will be handled in Chapter 4.

[3] As, for example, F. Loofs, *Symbolik*, 1902, p. 28, maintains.

[4] This is only an analogy, for the invocation of the " name ", with which baptism is accomplished, is not yet a baptismal symbol, though a reciprocal influence may be assumed.

only (Matt. 28: 19) is this name trinitarian; otherwise it is always that of Christ alone (Gal. 3: 2; 1 Cor. 1: 13; Acts 2: 38; 8: 16; 10: 48; 19: 5).

It is the same with the *confessions* in the New Testament. The overwhelming majority contain one article alone, the Christological; tripartite confessions are not yet to be found.[1] On the other hand, bipartite formulas are found, though much more seldom, which set the confession of God before that of Christ. Only later are tripartite formulas attested. This suggests the idea of a direct development of single-membered confessions into double-membered, and then further into triple-membered.

Yet we must not be misled into thinking that each step displaced its predecessor.[2] It is an established fact that formulas of one, two, and after a certain date three articles, contemporaneous and alongside one another, are attested from the earliest time. The New Testament proves this in the case of the single-membered formulas. The bipartite formula (God, Christ) is much *less frequent*, but its attestation is just as *old* as that of the others.

Tripartite formulas appear about 150, but the shorter symbols also remain in force at the same time. Thus the co-existence of one- and three-membered formulas appears in especially characteristic fashion in Irenæus: *Adv. Hær.* I, 10, 1: ". . . faith in *one* God, the Father almighty, Maker of heaven, earth, the sea and all that is therein; and in *one* Christ Jesus, the Son of God, who became flesh for our salvation; and in the Holy Spirit, who by the prophets revealed the plan of salvation and (double) advent (of Christ); and (who

---

[1] The trinitarian declarations in the New Testament (especially 2 Cor. 13: 13) have rather a liturgical character, and are not confessions of faith.

[2] R. Seeberg makes this supposition in too rigid a form in his article: " *Zur Geschichte der Entstehung des apostolischen Symbols* " in *ZKG*, New Series, III, 1922, p. 1 ff.

revealed) the virgin birth, the passion, the resurrection from the dead, the bodily ascension of the beloved Jesus Christ, our Lord, and His second coming from heaven in the glory of His Father for the restoration of all things, for the resurrection of all flesh of the whole of mankind . . . and for the just judgment of all. . . ."

This passage from Irenæus offers first of all an example of a short tripartite formula, in which each of the three almost equally long articles is symmetrically constructed. Of Christ, it says only this: *one* Christ Jesus, Son of God, become flesh for our salvation. In the third article, it speaks of the Holy Spirit only in so far as He by the prophets revealed the divine plan of salvation and rendered witness to Christ. This definition of the Spirit allows Irenæus to append to this article an independent confession in *one* article, which is purely Christological and more fully developed. He introduces it as a prophecy of the Spirit, although the preceding tripartite formula has already spoken of Christ. This text of Irenæus thus offers us a four-membered confession, in which faith in Christ is defined in two articles: first briefly comprised in the trinitarian scheme, then again in greater detail at the end. This skilful combination of Irenæus seems to us of the greatest importance for establishing historically how the external structure of the confession of faith has developed. We have here the decisive proof that there was a time when one- and three-membered formulas existed alongside one another, neither being renounced in favour of the other. Irenæus himself proves to us in another passage that bipartite and tripartite formulas coexisted. In *Adv. Hær.*, III, 1, 2; 4, 1-2, he mentions formulas which, like 1 Corinthians 8: 6, speak only of God and Christ, and are silent about the Holy Spirit. We find the same conjunction in Tertullian (*de Virg. Velandis*), where the confession contains only faith in

God and Christ, while elsewhere (*de Prœscr. Hœr.*, 13, *Adv. Praxeam*, 2) three articles are enumerated.[1]

We must here be on our guard likewise against arbitrary simplifications. For the early period, we have to admit a diversity of *contemporaneous* constructions.

With this reservation, it is still possible to establish a certain development, so far as formal construction is concerned. We saw that, in the New Testament, purely Christological formulas are by far the most frequent, bipartite are found seldom, and tripartite are altogether lacking. At a later date, Ignatius of Antioch still seems to know exclusively one-membered formulas,[2] but after him they are less frequent.[3] Three-membered formulas are for the first time[4] attested by Justin and in the *Epistola Apostolorum* (chap. 5),[5] that is only towards the middle of the second century. Hence it follows that a general development may be accepted, leading from the purely Christological formula up to formulas of several articles.[6] Yet the bipartite formula also goes back to the New Testament; it develops independently, and finally opens out into tripartite formulas, which gradually won the day over the others.

The originally most widespread Christian confession is quite certainly the *purely Christological* formula. This fact is as important for history as for theology. In the

[1] A further bipartite formula in Hippolytus, *Contra Noetum*, X, cf. Hahn, *op. cit.*, parag. 4.

[2] This appears certain, though it cannot be cogently proved. For in the anti-Docetist struggle he could have contented himself with the Christological passage of a *longer* confession. In any case, there is no trace in Ignatius of a confession of several articles.

[3] Later we find pure Christological formulas in the *Didascalia*, VI, 23, 8, and in the *Apostolic Constitutions*, VII, 36, 3.

[4] But the time of the first literary attestation is always quite considerably later than the composition itself.

[5] C. Schmidt, *Gespräche Jesu mit seinen Jüngern nach der Auferstehung (Texte und Untersuchungen*, 43), 1919. See below, p. 46, *n.* 2.

[6] Lietzmann has perhaps not taken this sufficiently into account. On the other hand, this is the germ of truth in the attempt of R. Seeberg (*op. cit.*) to trace an organic development.

earliest times, Christians regarded the confession of Christ as the essential of their faith. Faith in God was self-evident, and it they held in common with the Jews. When the centre of the Christian proclamation was to be affirmed, it seemed enough to give an exact expression of faith in Christ. The Old Testament, which alone formed Holy Scripture for the earliest community, had also to be read in the light of this confession. A close connection exists between this Christocentric perspective and the fact that most of the New Testament confessions are purely Christological. Proclamation of Christ is the *starting-point of every Christian confession*. The first place in the two- and three-membered formulas belongs indeed to God; but this should not mislead us into supposing that the essential element of Christian confession was faith in God.

Even where bipartite formulas are employed, one has the unambiguous impression that, in a *Christian* confession of faith, faith in God is really a function of faith in Christ. Thus in the bipartite confession cited by Polycarp in his letter, God is certainly named in the first place; but He is not confessed as Creator, but as He who *raised our Lord from the dead, and conferred majesty upon Him* (chap. 2). The one-membered confession cited by Ignatius in his letter to the Trallians (chap. 9), we have to understand as a preparatory step towards justifying the mention of God. At the end of this formula, in connection with the resurrection of Christ, the Father, in *genitivus absolutus*, is mentioned as the author of this action. If in the later symbols God is primarily named Father, it is chiefly as the Father of Christ.[1]

In the tripartite formulas, the Spirit is also very often determined through confession of Christ. On the

[1] It is particularly plain in the *Apostolic Constitutions*, VII, 41 (Hahn, parag. 129), where the trinitarian symbol is already developed, and where the first article runs: ". . . in one uncreated, only true God, the almighty, the *Father of Jesus Christ*."

one hand, He is described as the Paraclete sent by Christ (Tertullian, *Adv. Praxeam 2, Epist. apost.*[1]); on the other hand, the Christological sense is even more evident where the Spirit is spoken of only as He who announces Christ by the prophets. He thus appears in the first tripartite confession of which we have evidence; in that cited by Justin (*Apol.*, I, 31) He is called πνεῦμα προφητικόν; in that of *Apol.*, I, 61, He appears as He " who has announced by the prophets *everything that concerns Christ* ".[2] It is the same when Justin in *Apol.*, I, 31, introduces the confession of Christ with the words: " We find predicted by the prophets Him who is born of the Virgin. . . ."[3]

Similarly the confession of Tertullian (*de Præscr. Hær.*, 13) in the second article recalls that the Son was " *in nomine Dei varie visum a patriarchis, in prophetis semper auditum.*" Finally, the manner in which Irenæus in the passage already mentioned (I, 10, 1) associates the Christological confession with the tripartite confession[4] by means of the prophetic predictions of the Spirit concerning Christ, shows us how current was the Christological justification of the mention of the Spirit in the confession.

Thus we have established what was the *inner* motive for the transition from the confessions with one article to those with several. The demonstration confirms that

---

[1] Versions *L.* and *S.* only.

[2] Justin cites here the invocation of the name of the Trinity, as it belongs to Baptism. This invocation is clearly influenced by the text of the confession of faith.

[3] This Christological designation of the Spirit goes back perhaps to the ancient Christological confession of faith cited by Paul in the introduction to the Epistle to the Romans (1: 1-4): " the gospel of God (which he had promised afore by his prophets in the holy scriptures), concerning his Son, which was made of the seed of David according to the flesh; and declared to be the Son of God with power, according to the spirit of holiness, by the resurrection from the dead: Jesus Christ our Lord." In this ancient Christological confession, which assumes great importance for the development of the symbol, God is named, and the prophetic Spirit also included, but both as functions of Christ.

[4] See above, p. 36.

the ancient Church regarded the *proclamation of Christ as the essential element in all confessions.*

This simple confession expresses itself in the first place in short formulas: " *Kyrios Jesus Christos* " (1 Cor. 12: 3), " Jesus is the Christ " (1 John 2: 22), " Jesus is the Son of God " (Acts 8: 37, Western text; 1 John 4: 15; Heb. 4: 14), " Jesus is come in the flesh " (1 John 4: 2). Mention is also rightly made of the symbol of the fish, which is in fact a brief confession of Christ. The letters *IXΘΥΣ* correspond to the confession *'Ιησοῦς Χριστὸς Θεοῦ 'Υιὸς Σωτήρ.*[1]

Little by little, the short Christological confession developed along two lines: on the one hand, that attested in Romans 1: 3, where it is explained in the first place what Christ is *κατὰ σάρκα*, and then *κατὰ πνεῦμα* ; on the other hand, that of Philippians 2: 6 ff., the humiliation of Christ and His exaltation. The combination, according to the flesh—according to the spirit, appears yet again in 1 Peter 3: 18, perhaps also in 1 Timothy 3: 16, and in the confession quoted by Ignatius in his letter to the Smyrniots (chap. 1).[2] There it is already joined with the second pattern, which then acquires general currency; and on the lines of this pattern the majority of confessions from the earliest times are constructed, as in 1 Corinthians 15: 3 ff., Ignatius *ad Trall.*, 9, to mention only these.

We have still to ask which of the *external* situations, which we have described in the previous chapter, first rendered indispensable the use of a bipartite and then of a tripartite formula alongside of the Christological confession, which originally sufficed for the essential needs of the Church.

[1] For the importance of the fish symbol in the ancient Church, cf. inscriptions cited by F. Dölger, *Ichthys*, I, 248, 259 and 319.

[2] In place of *κατὰ πνεῦμα*, we read here *κατὰ θέλημα καὶ δύναμιν θεοῦ*, in which *δύναμις* is · probably borrowed from the confession of Rom. 1: 3 f.: *υἱοῦ θεοῦ ἐν δυνάμει κατὰ πνεῦμα ἁγιωσύνης.*

In the previous chapter we have in anticipation already suggested that the bipartite formulas owe their existence to the struggle against heathenism. The conversion of the heathen demanded that faith in God be enunciated before faith in Christ, in agreement with the Jewish confession of the oneness of God, the " Shema ".[1] It should be emphasised that the bipartite formulas in the New Testament appear precisely where a confession is opposed to heathenism: 1 Corinthians 8: 6 (things sacrificed to idols) and in the three passages of the Epistles to Timothy (1 Tim. 2: 5; 6: 13 f. 2 Tim. 4: 1f.), of which the second, as we have seen, pre-supposes appearance before the heathen authorities.

But dogmatic disputes also made bipartite formulas necessary. It is not by chance that Irenæus so willingly quotes bipartite formulas alongside of tripartite (*Adv. Hær.*, III, 1, 2; III, 4, 1-2; III, 16, 6). His whole theology is directed to proving, over against the Gnostics who denied the Creator God, the congruity of creation with redemption, of Creator with Redeemer. And the bipartite confession directed, according to Hippolytus, against the Modalist Noetus,[2] owes its origin to a dogmatic dispute, in which the effort was made to distinguish God and Christ against the Moda-list heresy which confused them.

The bipartite formula most current seems to be that quoted in 1 Corinthians 8: 6: " *One* God, from whom are all things, and we in him; and *one* Lord Jesus Christ, by whom are all things, and we by him." This formula indeed became the basis of all confessions with *several articles*.[3]

---

[1] J. Haussleiter, *Trinitarischer Glaube und Christusbekenntnis in der Alten Kirche*, 1920, according to R. Seeberg, *Dogmengeschichte* I, 2nd edn., p. 179, footnote, tried to prove that the Christological confession is Jewish-Christian only, while that with more than one article is heathen-Christian. The thesis in this hard and fast form cannot be maintained, in spite of an unassailable element of truth.

[2] Cf. Hahn, parag. 4.

[3] Cf. H. Lietzmann, *ZNW*, 1923, p. 268 ff., and also p. 272 f.

* * * But how did a tripartite confession arise out of a bipartite? We think it best to start from Ephesians 4: 4: "... *one* body, *one* Spirit, ... *one* hope, ... *one* Lord (*one* faith), *one* baptism, *one* God and Father of all, who is above all, and through all, and in all." In its present form the confession contains seven articles, which proclaim the unity of the Church. But at its base there appears to lie a confession in two articles, whose content is defined as in I Corinthians 8: 6: *one Kyrios*, and *one* God and Father of all things, and so on. But between mention of the *Kyrios* and of the Father a third expression (apart from that of " one faith ") is inserted: *one baptism*. Perhaps we have here the origin of the development from bipartite to tripartite formulas.

The employment of the confession in *baptism* made necessary a tripartite formula, in which the Spirit figures as the effect of baptism. We have already established[1] that even a one-membered formula, whenever it came to be employed as a baptismal symbol, had to mention baptism (I Peter 3: 20 ff.). In Ignatius (*Smyrn.*, I) this mention is made by speaking, in a purely Christological formula, of the baptism of Christ between virgin birth and crucifixion.

Accordingly mention of baptism is added to the bipartite formula of I Corinthians 8: 6. But the ἓν βάπτισμα of Ephesians 4: 4 could not be put on an equal footing with God the Father and God the Son as a third article of this symbol. So it is replaced by the *gift received in baptism*: the πνεῦμα. Thus a third article appears which can be set alongside the others on equality with them. This development was favoured by the ancient liturgical tripartite formulas existing independently of the confessions of faith (2 Cor. 13: 14), and by the triple invocation of the *name* in baptism, Matthew 28: 19, which properly speaking is not a

[1] See above, p. 20.

43

confession of faith. Later symbols conserved the ἕν before πνεῦμα˙ on the analogy of the εἷς θεός and the εἷς κύριος of I Corinthians 8: 6.[1]

We have seen that in earlier studies of the symbols too much importance is generally attributed to baptism in explaining the origin of the confessions of faith, and that it is often wrongly regarded as the only occasion of the formulation of a symbol. We have, however, ascertained that baptism can rightly claim a special place in the formation of *tripartite* formulas. In fact, the employment of a confession of faith at baptism resulted in the introduction of the Trinity, which from the earliest times appeared in other liturgical formulas as the formal principle of the confession. According as the employment of the confession was gradually limited to baptism, so the tripartite formula gained supremacy.[2]

The later symbols allow us to affirm further that the Spirit was named originally only as a *gift received in baptism.* In fact, the Spirit appears there in the third article in company with baptism. So in the symbol of Cyril of Jerusalem:[3] " and in *one* Holy Spirit, the Paraclete, who spoke by the prophets, and in *one* baptism of repentance for the forgiveness of sins, in *one* catholic Church, in the resurrection of the body and eternal life." So likewise in the two formulas transmitted by Epiphanius in the *Ancoratus*: in the shorter,[4] the third article ends thus: " We confess *one* baptism for the forgiveness of sins "; the second,[5] like the confession quoted by Ignatius (*ad Smyrn.*, 1), mentions also the baptism of Jesus in the Jordan: " and in the Holy Spirit, who spoke through the law, was preached by

---

[1] Cf. the symbols of Cæsarea (Hahn, *op. cit.*, parag. 123), of Cyril of Jerusalem (*op. cit.*, parag. 124), and of Nestorius (*op. cit.*, parag. 132).

[2] The symbol of the *Apostolic Constitutions*, VII, 41 (Hahn, *op. cit.*, parag. 129), is introduced with the words: πιστεύω καὶ βαπτίζομαι εἰς and particularly the third article: βαπτίζομαι καὶ εἰς πνεῦμα τὸ ἅγιον.

[3] Hahn, *op. cit.*, parag. 124.   [4] Hahn, *op. cit.*, parag. 125.

[5] Hahn, *op. cit.*, parag. 126.

the prophets, and descended at the Jordan . . ., and in one baptism of repentance." Similarly the confession of Nestorius[1] offers this form of the third article: ". . . and in the Holy Spirit, the Spirit of truth, who proceeds from the Father and imparts life, and in one catholic, holy and apostolic Church. We confess *one baptism for the forgiveness of sins*, one resurrection of the dead and one eternal life."

In the symbol of the *Apostolic Constitutions* (VII, 41)[2] baptism is not mentioned in this form. But the Spirit is introduced as having in view the Spirit conferred at baptism: " I was baptized also by the Holy Spirit, . . . who was finally sent for all who believe in the holy, catholic and apostolic Church."

In one of the most ancient tripartite formulas, of which the *Epistola Apostolorum* makes use,[3] the third article does not name baptism, but mentions along with the " holy Church " the *forgiveness of sins*. This element of the most ancient confessions of faith was introduced into the third article as a result of baptism. Formerly, in the purely *Christological* confessions, forgiveness of sins was mentioned in the affirmation concerning the *death of Christ*; I Cor. 15: 3: " died *for our sins* "; I Peter 3: 18: " Christ died *for our sins* "; I Tim. 2: 6: " who gave himself a ransom for all "; Ignatius to the Smyrniots (chap. 1): " under Pontius Pilate nailed in his flesh *for us*."[4] The displacement of the forgiveness of sins into the third article of the most ancient three-membered formulas shows anew that this third article owes its existence to baptism alone. For besides the

---

[1] Hahn, *op. cit.*, parag. 132.　　　　[2] See p. 44, *n.* 2.
[3] See p. 38, *n.* 5. For the partition into 5 members, see below, p. 46, *n.* 2.
[4] K. Holl in *Sitzungsbericht*, Berlin, 1919, p. 10, emphasizes rightly that, in the symbols with three articles, the forgiveness of sins refers only to the forgiveness received in baptism. But he has not noticed that, before the symbols quoted by him, there are yet more ancient confessions, which mention forgiveness only in connection with the death of Christ.

gift of the Spirit, the forgiveness of sins is the great work of baptism.[1]

Moreover, all that was included in this third article was regarded as the fruit of baptism, particularly the Church, originating in the baptism of the Spirit of Pentecost.[2]

The resurrection of the dead, once brought into connection with Christ through the Christological confessions (Ignatius, *ad Trall.*, 9), is henceforth regarded as a work of the Spirit (perhaps because of the passages I Corinthians 15: 42 ff. or Ezekiel 37: 1),[3] and is transferred to the third article.

In I Corinthians 8: 6, the prototype of confessions with more than one article, the first and second articles are both very short. But just as the third article slowly developed, so in time the first and second similarly received expansion. The most ancient tripartite formulas were short in both East and West. This is true also of the formula reconstructed by Lietzmann, attested in Egypt, which, according to him, certainly originates from Rome. It satisfies the need for liturgical symmetry, for each article contains only three members:[4]

I believe in God, the Father almighty,
And in Jesus Christ, His only begotten Son, our Lord,
And in the Holy Ghost, the Holy Church, the resurrection of the body.

[1] Mention of the *communio sanctorum*, which appears much later and only in Western symbols, is certainly to be connected with the sacraments (cf. with this τὰ ἄγια in *Didache*, IX, 5), to which the formula quoted by Hahn (*op. cit.*, parag. 74) and the symbol of Nîmes point. The mention of sacraments here supersedes that of baptism, as found in the ancient Eastern symbols.

[2] The partition of the symbol contained in the *Epistola Apostolorum* into five articles, parallel to the five breads, rests on a subsequent speculation of the author alone. It is not possible to stop here to prove that " Church " and " forgiveness of sins " were added to the symbol independently of the Spirit (against H. Lietzmann, *ZNW*, 1922, p. 22).

[3] Cf. Tertullian, *de Resurrectione Carnis*, 29 f.

[4] *Sitzungsbericht der Wissenschaften*, Berlin, 1919, Harnack, p. 112 f.; Lietzmann, p. 269 ff. Further, H. Lietzmann, " *Die Anfänge des Glaubensbekenntnisses* " in *Festgabe zu Harnacks 70. Geburtstag*, 1921, p. 226 f.

In East and West, the second article of this confession was developed further. But the procedure was not that of Irenæus,[1] who had contented himself with appending to the tripartite confession a longer Christological formula. Instead, the expansion was incorporated in *the second article of this tripartite confession*, so that it became considerably longer.

This development, however, we shall not follow here. It is the creative period that alone occupies us in this study, and it is sufficient for us to know the circumstances and ways in which the first confessional formulas originated.

We find here the result of our Chapter 2 confirmed: *the life of the whole primitive Church* determined not only the content but also *the formal construction* of the earliest confessions. We have seen that the central confession in apostolic and post-apostolic times consisted in what later formed the second article. But the needs of the life of the Church from the beginning favoured the development of confessions with several articles, and finally led to a formula constructed on trinitarian lines. And yet, through its connection with the originally independent Christological symbol, the Christocentric character was preserved.

It is as if, when the Christian faith was being summarized in a symbol, there were a pre-established harmony between the outward circumstances, which we have ascertained, and the inner content of the symbol itself. Such an agreement was only possible because the first confessions of faith were not the product of the private opinion of an author, but the spontaneous creative act of the primitive Church.

[1] See above, p. 37.

Chapter 4

THE ESSENCE OF THE CHRISTIAN FAITH ACCORDING TO THE EARLIEST CONFESSIONS

IN the foregoing chapters we have treated the source of the first confessions of faith as a problem of the history of primitive Christianity. We have now further to set the question within the framework of the history of Christian *dogma*, and from this standpoint to examine the essentials *common* to the oldest formulas. We look, that is, for what the first generations unanimously regarded as the essential content of the Gospel which they handed down to us in detailed form in the books of the New Testament. This question is of vital interest for every Christian theology, since on it depends the much debated definition of the " essence of Christianity ".

We have said that there is, as it were, a pre-established harmony between the circumstances which influenced the forming of the first symbols and the nature of their contents. In fact, in every situation which we have examined,[1] the same essential question presented itself: how is the evangelical Gospel to be summarized ? Certainly this question was subordinated to the necessities of the Church, so that the answer was suited to the various immediate needs of the primitive community, and thus emerged in correspondingly various forms. It is all the more important to establish from certain points of view *an essential unanimity* between the various formulas of the first and second centuries, in spite of the diverse contemporary circumstances which called them into being. This una-

[1] See Chapter 2, p. 18 ff.

nimity proves that the needs of the Church, while influencing the statement of truth by the earliest confessions at their origin, were not a source of error.

To what extent can we say this of the development in the second century, which under the influence of historical circumstances has the tendency to expand further the short Christological formulas of earliest times, and then opens out into the tripartite confession? This evolution does not *a priori* represent a necessarily erroneous development. In particular, faith in God the Father and in the Holy Ghost really constitutes a part of the essential substance of faith in Christ, who stands as the sole object of confession in the majority of the earliest formulas. But the more the confession expands with time, the greater is the danger of a displacement of the centre of gravity, and the problem which had made a summary necessary *reappears*. The more exact and complete the confession is, the greater the need of an exposition alongside of it; and the question which arose in the case of Scripture arises now in the case of the symbol itself: what is the central content of faith, from which the other contents of faith must be explicated?

What is to be the answer to this? Only the historical development, as we have traced it in the foregoing chapters, can provide us with the ground for an objective answer. It alone gives us the key which allows us to say in what sense the authors of the New Testament interpreted the more developed Credos. For this purpose, it is enough to know the kernel from which arose the further forms. This historical kernel is at the same time the dogmatic kernel. *The points in common*, which are regularly repeated in the oldest formulas, however short they may be, represent the essential elements of the evangelical Gospel as the earliest Christians understood it.

* * * When we state our question in this way, one of the results of our historical examination acquires importance of the first rank. We remind ourselves that the earliest Christian writings contain pure Christological confessions, along with a few formulas which mention Christ and at the same time God the Father. In *all* confessions of the apostolic age the concern is with Christ, while God is not mentioned in all. Since, then, the first class forms the overwhelming majority, there emerges a first conclusion which becomes important for the recognition of the dogmatic kernel of all confessions: the starting and middle point of Christian faith is faith in Christ.

From this standpoint, we affirm that the development of the Christological formulas in spite of all into a final tripartite form falsified the exposition of the essence of Christianity. The source of the error in this case is certainly not the *fact itself* of mentioning the Father and the Holy Ghost; on the contrary, we have seen that these articles of faith are an integral and essential part of faith in Christ. Rather it is the *position* which is assigned in all future symbols to the various articles of the confessions so shaped that leads to a falsification of the perspective. Thus in fact, God the Father holds the first place in the future symbols, before any mention of the Son. This corresponds certainly to the logical connection between human ideas of Father and Son. But this order threatens to suggest the Jewish representation of Christ, to which the doctrine of the whole New Testament runs contrary, that one must set out from faith in God the Father in order to reach faith in Christ. Against this, the Christian maintains, according to the doctrine of the New Testament, that he reaches God through Christ. The thought of the New Testament is strongly Christocentric: Christ is the divine Mediator and is nearer man; His person is the central object of faith.

From this point of view, the tripartite formula of 2 Corinthians 13: 13, which sets the grace of the Lord Jesus Christ before the love of God the Father, is in closer conformity with the whole of the New Testament witness than that of Matthew 28: 19, which, under the influence of liturgical rhythm and logic, or because the Son Himself is the speaker, sets God the Father before God the Son. Among the rare confessions of the New Testament containing more than one article, there is besides only one—Ephesians 4: 5 f.—which speaks of the *Kyrios* before it speaks of God: *one* Lord (*one* faith), *one* baptism, *one* God and Father of all.

In the very old bipartite formula, indeed, which the Apostle Paul employs in 1 Corinthians 8: 6, we find the Father " of whom are all things, and we in him " mentioned before the Lord Jesus Christ, " by whom are all things, and we by him ". But it is characteristic that even here the two are not yet separated, as in the later Credos. These, while they speak in the first article only of the creation, separate perhaps too much the function of God from that of Christ, and so give rise to the false conception that, according to the New Testament, Christ has nothing to do with the creation.[1] The confession of 1 Corinthians 8: 6 reminds us on the contrary that Christ, while He is the Mediator for men, is also Mediator for the whole of creation, answering to the rôle which man plays in the divine creation according to Genesis. In this, the confession of 1 Corinthians 8: 6 concurs with the doctrine of the Epistle to the Colossians (1: 16): " for by him were all things created, that are in heaven, and that are in earth, visible and invisible, whether they be thrones, or dominions, or principalities, or powers: all things were created by him, and for him: and he is *before* all things, and by him all things consist." The formula of 1 Corinthians 8: 6

---

[1] The controversy between Karl Barth and Emil Brunner over natural revelation could be traced back to this problem.

agrees besides with the Johannine prologue: " all things were made by him "; and with that of the Epistle to the Hebrews (1 : 2 f.): " by whom also he made the worlds."

To remain true to the spirit of the confession, every exposition of the Credo must set out from the Christological article, and from there proceed to the first and third articles, regardless of the order in which the articles follow each other. There is reason to subject the interpretations of the Credos, which have been given in the course of the centuries, to examination in this connection. Since the believer of the first century believed in the *Kyrios Christos*, he believed also in God and in the Holy Ghost. It is interesting to remind ourselves at this point of the attempts we have noted to create a Christological connection within the bipartite and tripartite confessions, in order to link the expressions about God and the Holy Ghost with that about Christ. Thus we have seen that the symbol of Ignatius (*Trall.*, 9) in its conclusion introduces the Father as He " who has raised Christ ". Similarly, the symbol mentioned in the *Letter of Polycarp* (chap. 2, 1 f.) shows us the Father, whom it mentions at the beginning, not as Creator, but as He " who raised our Lord Jesus Christ from the dead, and has given Him glory and the throne at His right hand ". It is as the Father of Christ that God is named " Father ".

Similarly the earliest confessions, which under the influence of their employment in baptism subjoin the Holy Ghost, justify their mention of Him likewise in a Christological way:[1] the Holy Ghost, who has spoken through the prophets, in order to announce Christ; so Justin, *Apol.*, I, 61 (πνεύματος ἁγίου ὁ διὰ τῶν προφητῶν προεκήρυξε τὰ κατὰ τὸν Ἰησοῦν πάντα), 31 and 13; Irenæus, *Adv. Hær.*, I, 10, 1; and Tertullian, *de Præscr. Hær.*, 13.

Consequently we must not let ourselves be deceived by the apparent independence of one another in which

[1] Cf. *supra*, Chapter 3, p. 39.

the three articles find themselves in the later tripartite symbols.

In another connection again, the partition of the various elements of the more developed symbols tends to weaken the Christocentric character of the primitive conception. We saw[1] how the originally independent Christological confession was at a definite time inserted into the second article of a short and at first symmetrical trinitarian confession. The text of the Christological formula suffered no great transformation in consequence of this insertion into the tripartite confession; but an important element of the old Christological symbol was thereby relegated to the third article: the forgiveness of sins.[2] It was thus subordinated to the affirmations about the Holy Ghost, and we have seen that this itself entered into the confession in close connection with the sacrament of baptism. In thus connecting the forgiveness of sins and baptism closely together, and in later moving them into proximity with the mention of the Church, the later Credo introduced a conception certainly not strange to the New Testament; but it here again *displaced the centre of gravity*. For according to the New Testament and the New Testament confessions, the forgiveness of sins was accomplished once for all by Christ on the Cross, before it is offered to men in baptism.

So the Christological formula of 1 Corinthians 15: 3: ἀπέθανεν ὑπὲρ τῶν ἁμαρτιῶν ἡμῶν; that of 1 Peter 3: 18: Χριστὸς ἅπαξ περὶ ἁμαρτιῶν ἀπέθανεν; that of 1 Timothy 2: 6: ὁ δοὺς ἑαυτὸν ἀντίλυτρον ὑπὲρ πάντων. The more detailed symbol cited by Ignatius (*Smyrn.*, 1) similarly adds to the mention of the crucifixion of Christ (καθηλωμένον) under Pontius Pilate and Herod the words ὑπὲρ ἡμῶν; and the allusion to the forgiveness of sins

[1] *Vide supra*, Chapter 3, p. 47.
[2] K. Holl mentions this: " *Zur Auslegung des 2. Artikels des sogenannten apostolischen Glaubensbekenntnisses* " in *Sitzungsbericht der Berliner Akademie der Wissenschaften*, 1919, p. 2 ff.

53

accomplished by the death of Christ was still conserved in the second article of certain later tripartite
formulas of the East. Thus the Nicæno-Constantino-
politan Symbol says σταυρωθέντα δὲ ὑπὲρ ἡμῶν, though
in the third article the ἄφεσις ἁμαρτιῶν is again mentioned in connection with baptism.[1] But in the
predominant type of Eastern symbol, and above all
in the old Roman symbol, prototype of the so-called
Apostles' Creed, only in the third article is anything
said of the forgiveness of sins, and its mention in the
second is suppressed. We have established a similar
development in connection with the resurrection of the
dead, which originally was closely linked with the
resurrection of Christ (Ignatius, ad Trall., 11, 23). At
these points, corroboration is again found for the view
already expressed. The partition of the material in
the detailed symbols tends to weaken the strongly
Christocentric character, in which we discerned the
essential principle of the primitive confession.

We have now to seek for the central element of this
Christological confession itself. For this, we follow the
same procedure as above: we reduce the formulas of
the earliest time to their common elements, and go back
to the shortest formulas.

In agreement with K. Holl,[2] we are of opinion that
the whole second article of the future Apostles' Creed
has this aim only, to explain the two expressions
mentioned at the beginning of this symbol: υἱὸς
μονογενής and κύριος. For the first this is done in the
sentence speaking about the conception by the Holy
Ghost and the virgin birth, and for the second in

---

[1] In other symbols of the East, the ὑπὲρ ἡμῶν is not connected with
the forgiveness of sins, but is brought into conjunction with the in-
carnation of Christ: cf. Nicene Creed: δι' ἡμᾶς τοὺς ἀνθρώπους καὶ διὰ
τὴν ἡμετέραν σωτηρίαν κατελθόντα. But cf. also the symbol in Irenæus
already frequently mentioned, Adv. Hær., I, 10, 1: σαρκωθέντα ὑπὲρ τῆς
ἡμῶν σωτηρίας.
[2] Article cited above, p. 53, n. 2.

54

the sentence speaking of the suffering, death, burial, resurrection, ascension, elevation to the right hand of God, and the second coming. We do not stop to consider the much more ill-founded considerations which Karl Holl adds to this correct assertion. We will retain the latter, but seek to give it a better foundation, thanks to the results of our study of the prehistory of the future Apostles' Creed.

Among the shortest formulas of the New Testament we have especially singled out these two: " Jesus Christ is the *Kyrios* " (1 Cor. 12: 3) and " Jesus is the Son of God " (Acts 8: 37, Heb. 4: 14, and 1 John 4: 15). These two expressions are already combined in Romans 1: 3: " Jesus Christ our Lord, his Son, which was made of the seed of David, according to the flesh; and declared to be the Son of God with power, according to the spirit of holiness, by the resurrection from the dead." This confession is constructed according to the pattern κατὰ σάρκα—κατὰ πνεῦμα. The first part (κατὰ σάρκα) concerns the birth of Christ, the second (κατὰ πνεῦμα) His redemption. The first moves in the sphere of the expression ὁ υἱὸς τοῦ θεοῦ, the second in that of the synonymous expressions υἱὸς τοῦ θεοῦ ἐν δυνάμει and κύριος. By His Davidic birth Christ is manifested as Son of God, by His resurrection as Son of God *with power*, or, what is the same thing, as *Kyrios*. The two titles are also united, though in reverse order, in the short formula of 2 Timothy 2: 8: " Jesus Christ is risen from the dead, of the seed of David." Philippians 2: 6 ff. again speaks on the one hand of the divine origin of Christ (ἐν μορφῇ θεοῦ), which here indeed is not explained κατὰ σάρκα. On the other it speaks of His work as servant which culminates in His elevation to the rank of *Kyrios-Adonai*, a name which is above all names, since it formerly belonged to God alone. So also the different formulas cited in whole or in part by Ignatius of Antioch speak

55

first of the Divine Sonship of Christ. Nor is this explained only by His Davidic origin as in Romans 1: 3, but at the same time by His virgin birth and His procession from the Holy Ghost.[1] In the second place they enumerate the decisive facts of the Christological drama which culminates in the resurrection.

The second coming of Christ is not yet regularly mentioned in the earliest confessions. The Aramaic formula "*maranatha*", though from the philological point of view it can be read as indicative, "the Lord comes", appears, according to the Greek translation in Revelation 22: 20, to be rather an imperative: "our Lord, come !" It is, then, probably a prayer and not a confession. The first mention of future judgment exercised by Christ which we find in a confession is the formula of 2 Timothy 4: 1: " I charge thee therefore before God and the Lord Jesus Christ, who shall judge the quick and the dead at his appearing."[2] If the announcement of the second coming is rather rare in the first confessions, this does not mean that it plays no rôle at all among the cardinal ideas of the first generations. But it does mean that the hope of the second coming of Christ is for them *included* in the certainty

---

[1] *Eph.*, 18, 2: ἐκυοφορήθη ὑπὸ Μαρίας κατ᾽ οἰκονομίαν θεοῦ ἐκ σπέρματος μὲν Δαβίδ, πνεύματος δὲ ἁγίου. *Smyrn.*, 1, 1: ἐκ γένους Δαβίδ κατὰ σάρκα, υἱὸν θεοῦ κατὰ θέλημα καὶ δύναμιν θεοῦ (corresponding to the Holy Ghost) γεγεννημένον ἀληθῶς ἐκ παρθένου. *Trall.*, 9: τοῦ ἐκ γένους Δαβίδ τοῦ ἐκ Μαρίας.

The juxtaposition of Davidic ancestry and virgin birth for explaining the divine Sonship of Christ according to the flesh was possible thanks to the theory, widely held in the second century, that Mary herself belonged to the stem of David: cf. especially *Syr. sin.* and *Diatessaron* at Luke 2: 4; *Protevg. Jac.*, 10, 1; Justin, *Dial.*, 43, 45; Irenæus, *Adv. Hær.*, III, 21, 5; III, 26, 1; Tertullian, *Adv. Marc.*, III, 17.

In *Eph.*, 18, 2 and *Smyrn.*, 1, 1, the old general principle for dividing the confession κατὰ σάρκα—κατὰ πνεῦμα (cf. Rom. 1: 3 and 1 Peter 3: 18 f.) serves only to distinguish the different elements of the divine origin of Christ: His Davidic ancestry and the virgin birth as κατὰ σάρκα, and the conception by the Holy Ghost as κατὰ πνεῦμα (in *Smyrn.*, 1, 1: κατὰ θέλημα καὶ δύναμιν θεοῦ).

[2] Is the allusion to judgment of the quick and the dead in 1 Peter 4: 5 perhaps to be taken as a reminder of an eschatological deduction from the formula employed in the preceding chapter ?

56

of His resurrection and elevation to the right hand of God already accomplished. In general it seemed unnecessary in a short summary to include a special mention of the expectation of the second coming. The culminating point of the second part of the Christological confession was in most cases the resurrection, and elevation of Christ; only later, in the second century, was it accorded an eschatological conclusion.

Accordingly we can conclude that the divine Sonship of Jesus Christ and His elevation to the dignity of *Kyrios*, as consequence of His death and resurrection, are the two essential elements in the majority of the confessions of the first century.

* * * But we can go yet further. In reducing the summary of the confession of faith of the earliest Christians even more, we can try to arrive at the central principle at the heart of the Christian confession. That is, we have to ask whether the divine Sonship and the elevation to the dignity of the *Kyrios* form so to say two poles independent of one another. Examination of the formulas of the first and second centuries prove that this is not so.

First of all, we affirm that the divine Sonship, though it figures in most of the first Christian confessions, is yet lacking in certain of them. This is so in 1 Corinthians 15: 3 ff., where all the elements have the resurrection in view,[1] as also in 1 Peter 3: 18 ff., 1 Timothy 3: 16 and 2 Timothy 4: 1. On the other hand, the resurrection and the exaltation are never lacking, and this justifies us in supposing that even in the short formula Ἰησοῦς Χριστός ὁ υἱὸς τοῦ θεοῦ the thought is above all of the υἱὸς τοῦ θεοῦ ἐν δυνάμει (cf. Rom. 1: 4). The centre

---

[1] Of course the Apostle could be contenting himself in this chapter on the question of the resurrection with mentioning that part which referred to the resurrection. Thus it would be in principle possible that he has here cited only a part of a more detailed confession. It is, however, more probable that he has chosen a formula which had as its sole object precisely the resurrection following upon death and burial.

and culmination of the confession is Christ exalted to the right hand of God. It is not the divine Sonship that, serves to explain the exaltation of the risen Christ; rather, setting out from the dignity of Christ as the resurrected, *Kyrios*, the Christian of the first century speaks of Christ's divine origin and later of His second coming. Thus the formula in 2 Timothy 2: 8 (μνημόνευε Ἰησοῦν Χριστόν ἐγηγερμένον ἐκ νεκρῶν, ἐκ σπέρματος Δαβίδ, κατὰ τὸ εὐαγγέλιόν μου) mentions the resurrection before His Davidic origin. If the other confessions place the origin of Christ in chronological order before His resurrection and exaltation, this does not compel us to regard the first as more important. Just as little should the place accorded to God the Father before God the Son make us forget that for the earliest Christians faith in God is in reality a function of their faith in Christ.

Thus the confession of Philippians 2: 6 ff. is so constructed that from the beginning onwards everything is viewed retrospectively under the aspect of the Christ "highly exalted", to whom God has given the name "which is above every name". It finds its culmination in the confession *Kyrios Christos*, which "to the glory of God, every tongue should confess" of all things "in heaven and on earth and under the earth". It is evident that this short formula was the starting-point of the more detailed confession which the Apostle cites in Philippians 2: 6 ff.

It is, then, the *present* Lordship of Christ, inaugurated by His resurrection and exaltation to the right hand of God, that is the centre of the faith of primitive Christianity. The affirmation of the present reign of Christ, and of the power in heaven and on earth conferred upon Him, is the historical and dogmatic core of the Christian confession, which we were to seek. Its simplest expression is the formula *Kyrios Christos*. We have seen that it was pronounced in the persecution before heathen magistrates,[1] in the liturgy at divine service,[2] and in exorcism;[3] and the cardinal importance of this confession becomes plain when we find that the Apostle Paul in Romans 10: 9, speaking of " confession with the mouth " *in general,* can write: " confess that Jesus is the Christ."

The affirmation *Kyrios Jesus Christos* means that Christ rules as King, not only over men, but also over all invisible powers " in heaven, and on earth, and under the earth ". It is the same conviction which in another connection is expressed in the Christological interpretation of Psalm 110, where it is proclaimed that the King will sit at the right hand of God, and " all enemies " will be conquered and subjected to Him. These " enemies " are identified in the Christian scheme[4] with the invisible powers, and regarded as earlier rulers of the world. Their subjection marks the victory already accomplished through the death and resurrection of Christ, and also the real beginning of the reign of Christ. This reign passes beyond the limits of the community of the faithful, and comprises the whole world; and yet the invisible powers, which are only bound and subject to Christ, must be again and finally vanquished, in order to pass at the end of time to their appointed annihilation.[5]

Since the present lordship of the *Kyrios Christos* is inseparable from the subjection of the " powers ", most of the developed confessions of early times are not content to say that Christ sits at the right hand of God; they emphasize with characteristic regularity the subjection of the invisible powers under Him. Here again we have to refer to the confession of Philippians 2: 6 ff.,

[1] Cf. Chapter 2, p. 25 f.   [2] Cf. Chapter 2, p. 21 f.   [3] Cf. Chapter 2, p. 23 f.
[4] 1 Cor. 15: 25; Eph. 1: 21 f.; Heb. 10: 13; 1 Peter 3: 22; Acts 2: 34; Matt. 22: 44; Mark 12: 30; Luke 20: 42; 1 *Clem.*, 36, 5; *Barn.*, 12, 10.
[5] Cf. O. Cullmann, *Königsherrschaft Christi und Kirche im Neuen Testament*, Zollikon, 1941.

which reaches its climax in the formula *Kyrios Christos*. To make it clear that this formula has in view the complete sovereignty of Christ over all other earthly κύριοι and the invisible powers which stand behind them, it is pronounced in Philippians 2: 11 by precisely these powers themselves, whose " every knee should bow ", and by every tongue of things in heaven, and on earth, and under the earth.

The confession of 1 Peter 3: 22 says: " who is gone into heaven, and is on the right hand of God; *angels and authorities and powers being made subject unto him* " (ὑποταγέντων αὐτῷ ἀγγέλων καὶ ἐξουσιῶν καὶ δυνάμεων).

The formula of 1 Timothy 3 : 16 alludes to the angelic powers: "seen of angels ".[1] The one cited in the *Epistle of Polycarp* (chap. 2, 1) does not forget to add, after mentioning the resurrection, that the " glory and the throne at God's right hand are assigned to Christ ", and that to Him " all heavenly and earthly beings are subject, and everything which breathes serves him " (ᾧ ὑπετάγη τὰ πάντα ἐπουράνια καὶ ἐπίγεια, ᾧ πᾶσα πνοὴ λατρεύει). The more matured confession of Ignatius of Antioch (*Trall.*, 9, 1) clearly exhibits the regularity with which the ἐπουράνια, the ἐπίγεια, and the ὑποχθόνια appear in the oldest symbols: ". . . he was crucified and died, *the beings in heaven and on earth and under the earth saw him* " (βλεπόντων τῶν ἐπουρανίων καὶ ἐπιγείων καὶ ὑποχθονίων). Ignatius put the Christological formula transmitted to him at the service of his polemic against the Docetists. Hence he here makes the powers *witnesses* of the reality of the death and the bodily resurrection of Christ. But it is apparent that originally here, as in the earlier confessions, the only thing that matters is their subjection.

---

[1] The continuation, " preached unto the Gentiles ", alludes probably to Christ's preaching to the dead. This preaching is thus mentioned before the ascension. The descent into hell is brought into connection on the one hand with the preaching to the dead (1 Peter 3: 18 f.), and on the other with the conquest of the powers of hades (*Symbol of Sirmium*, cf. Hahn, *op. cit.*, parag. 163).

The fact that Ignatius retained mention of these powers, while assigning them a new rôle, confirms that we are dealing here with a *constant and central* element in all confessions of the first century. Even in the middle of the second century we find traces of this. The confession cited by Justin in the *Dialogue with Trypho* (chap. 85) names Christ: κύριος τῶν δυνάμεων. Alluding to exorcisms, in view of which confession is made of this *Kyrios*, " crucified under Pontius Pilate, risen from the dead, and ascended into heaven ", Justin adds that its recital implies even now *the subjection of every demon* (πᾶν δαιμόνιον ἐξορκιζόμενον νικᾶται καὶ ὑποτάσσεται). It is apparent that Justin, like Ignatius, employs here a formula which connects the victory over the invisible powers with Christ's ascension. The lordship of the Kyrios is possible only on this condition. In the formula of the *First Apology* of Justin (chap. 42), after mention of crucifixion, death and ascension, there follows the word ἐβασίλευσεν: He assumed royalty.

The declarations "Christ reigns ", " the powers are subject unto him ", " he sits at the right hand of God ", are only different ways of expressing the same fact in the faith of the earliest Christians. This fact found its shortest expression in the formula *Kyrios Christos.*

In the long confession of Irenæus (*Adv. Hær.*, I, 10, 1) which we have already examined in a different connection, we again find the ἐπουράνια, the ἐπίγεια and the καταχθόνια. After mention of the second coming, we find the passage from Philippians 2: 10 incorporated: " every knee " of these powers bows, and " every tongue " confesses "*Kyrios Jesus Christos*". It is true that the homage rendered by these powers to Christ as sign of their subjection is here placed in the eschatological future. This " deferment " must certainly be ascribed to Irenæus, for it conforms to the general tendency of his thought. In his combat against the

Gnostic heresy, Irenæus exaggerated, as one may say, in such a way as to overemphasize the absolutely rectilinear character of the development, which leads from the creation to the completion of the messianic times. The usual view is that in the present Kingdom of Christ the powers are already conquered and subjected. Yet, while they await their annihilation at the end of time, they do not meantime lose the possibility of again disengaging themselves temporarily from the bonds which attach them to their master Christ. In Irenæus' system there is no place for the Kingdom of Christ so conceived. For this reason he takes account only of the eschatological subjection of the powers.

The Christians of the first generation, on the contrary, believe in the eschatological triumph of Christ, because they believe in the triumph already won by Him. They believe in the future Kingdom of God because they believe in the present reign of Christ.[1] We have seen[2] that this is the reason why there is as yet no need to make special mention of the hope in the earliest summaries of faith: it is included in the certainty of the present reign of Christ: *Kyrios Christos!* The divine origin of Christ, His birth and His second coming are seen, then, wholly in the light of the mission which He presently fulfils, in virtue of the divine plan. The contents of belief relating to God and the Holy Ghost are only the unfolding of faith in Christ. Similarly what the first Christians have to say about Christ Himself proceeds from the certainty that Christ is the *Kyrios*, that, since His triumph over the visible and invisible powers, He reigns.

[1] The consequences of this assertion for the whole eschatological problem of the New Testament are indicated in O. Cullmann, *Christus und die Zeit*.
See above, p. 56 f.

CONCLUSION

WE have examined the development of the earliest confessions to find what was the essence of the faith of the earliest Christians. The essence thus revealed concerns the central ideas of the New Testament which are of *direct* interest to men: Christ, who in virtue of His divine mission is near to man, or more exactly, Christ, who already exercises His divine reign *now*.

So we believe that we have really found the core of all the confessions of faith of primitive Christianity. Is it to be regretted that the ancient Church, under the influence of historical circumstances and internal necessities, did not confine itself to this short and concise formula, which was content to proclaim the present Lordship of Christ ? We do not think so. The position is, indeed, that (i) the more developed confessions, as was said, weakened the Christocentric character of the faith of the New Testament; and that (ii) they have to be interpreted in the light of this original formula, whose importance for the historical and theological understanding of Christian doctrine we have affirmed. But on the other hand it must also be said that this short formula had necessarily to be expanded.

Certainly it is necessary to know that the historical starting point and dogmatic centre of Christian faith is faith in Jesus Christ. But it is also necessary to know that this faith, so far from excluding faith in God the Father, on the contrary gives faith in God the Father its Christian foundation. With the Holy Ghost, the case is the same.

On the other hand, when the earliest Christians confess that Christ is the Lord, this is a precise declaration of the time when it pleased God to reveal His plan of salvation: the time which comprises, not only the present, but also the past and the future. If Christ is Lord today, this is because yesterday He became flesh and was crucified, and because tomorrow He will come again to judge the quick and the dead. The confession " Christ is Lord " includes reference to the earthly work of Christ, and also to His second coming, which at the same time it invokes.

The divine plan of salvation embraces the present, but a present bound to the past and the future. This plan unfolds itself in the linear time of the Bible, which has nothing to do with the Greek conception of cyclic time. This is so, because the divine plan, according to Christian faith, is wholly Christological: " Christ, the same yesterday, and today, and for ever " (Heb. 13: 8). Christian faith does not reduce to an affirmation about the past alone; this would lead straight to a " historism " which impaired the Biblical conception of linear time. Neither does it reduce to an affirmation about the future alone; this would lead straight to an apocalyptic which, in contrast to the Biblical eschatology, tended to separate hope and faith. Christianity is true to its origins in ascribing first-rank importance in its strictly Christological plan of salvation to the present as a time of grace. The danger of isolating past or future is then excluded. The course of the Christian revelation becomes clear: past and future are connected by the present, which is the time intervening between the resurrection and the second coming of Christ, the time in which already Christ invisibly exercises His Lordship. .

Made in United States
Troutdale, OR
03/10/2024

18360696R00040